THE LOSS OF JAPAN'S
SECRET WEAPON!

THE
KATA
FACTOR

Japan May Lose Steam
As Younger Generations
Take Over!

Boye Lafayette De Mente

A Phoenix BOOKS ORIGINAL

Other Books by the Author

[Books on China]
The Chinese Mind—Understanding Traditional Chinese
Beliefs and their Influence on Contemporary Culture
Reveal the Culture and Mindset of the Chinese]
Chinese in Plain English
Survival Chinese & Instant Chinese
Etiquette Guide to China—Know the Rules that
Make the Difference
CHINA – Understanding & Dealing with the Chinese Way
Of Doing Business

[Books on Japan]
JAPAN – Understanding & Dealing with the New Japanese
Way of Doing Business
KATA—The Key to Understanding & Dealing
with the Japanese
Japan's Cultural Code Words
The Japanese Have a Word for It!
Mistress-Keeping in Japan
Exotic Japan—The Sensual & Visual Pleasures
Discovering Cultural Japan
Business Guide to Japan
Japanese in Plain English
**Speak Japanese Today—A Little Language
Goes a Long Way!**
Instant Japanese & Survival Japanese
Japan Made Easy—All You Need to Know to Enjoy Japan
Dining Guide to Japan
Shopping Guide to Japan
Etiquette Guide to Japan—Know the Rules that
Make the Difference
The Japanese Samurai Code—Classic Strategies for Success

YOUNGER GENERATIONS LOSING STEAM!

Japan Unmasked—The Character & Culture of the Japanese
Elements of Japanese Design—Understanding & Using
Japan's Classic *Wabi-Sabi-Shibui* Concepts
Sex and the Japanese—The Sensual Side of Japan
Samurai Strategies—42 Secret Martial Arts from
Musashi's "Book of Five Rings"
Why the Japanese are a Superior People—The Advantages
of Using Both Sides of Your Brain!
Amazing Japan—Why Japan is one of the World's
Most Intriguing Countries
Exotic Japan—The Sensual & Visual Pleasures
SABURO—The Saga of a Teenage Samurai in
17th Century Japan
THE KATA FACTOR! Japan's Secret Weapon!

[Books on Korea]
Korean Business Etiquette
Korean in Plain English
Korea's Business & Cultural Code Words
Etiquette Guide to Korea— Know the Rules that
Make the Difference
Instant Korean
Survival Korean

[Books on Mexico]
Why Mexicans Think & Behave the Way They Do—
The Cultural Factors that Created the Character & Personality
of the Mexican People
THE MEXICAN MIND – Understanding & Appreciating
Mexican Culture
Romantic Mexico—The Image & the Realities

[Other Titles]

YOUNGER GENERATIONS LOSING STEAM!

Which Side of Your Brain Am I Talking To? – The
Advantages
of Using Both Sides of Your Brain
How to Measure the Sexuality of Men & Women by
Their Facial Features
Samurai Principles & Practices that will Help Preteens &
Teens in School, Sports, Social Activities
& Choosing Careers
Romantic Hawaii—Sun, Sand, Surf & Sex
Women of the Orient
Asian Face Reading—Unlock the Secrets Hidden
in the Human Face
Why Ignorance, Stupidity and Violence Plague Mankind
How to Measure the Sexuality of Men & Women by
Their Facial Features
Bridging Cultural Barriers in China, Japan, Korea & Mexico
Brave New World of American Sex!
ONCE A FOOL—From Japan to Alaska by
Amphibious Jeep
THE ORIGINS OF HUMAN VIOLENCE! – Male
Dominance, Ignorance, Religions & Willful Stupidity!
Why Oriental Girls Attract Western Men!

See my website: BoyeDeMente.com

*All titles available from Amazon
and other online booksellers

**Some of my Japan titles also available in Chinese, Czech,
French, German, Hebrew, Italian, Indonesian, Japanese,
Polish,
Portuguese, Russian & Spanish editions.

CONTENTS

Introduction:
WHAT MAKES THE JAPANESE *JAPANESE?*

By any standard, the Japanese have traditionally been a superior people. Their almost unbelievable success in turning a small chain of resource poor islands into one of the greatest economic powers the world has ever seen *in less than three decades* is proof of that. The fact that the "Miracle of Japan" would not have happened without significant contributions from the United States and Western Europe, along with a variety of other external factors, certainly tempers but does not negate the accomplishments of the Japanese.

Japan's early history was, in fact, a continuing record of extraordinary accomplishments, beginning with its transformation from a feudalistic kingdom of sword-carrying warriors, shopkeepers and peasants in 1868 to a world-class military power by 1895. The special character and ability of the Japanese was recognized by more astute Western visitors even before Japan's feudal age ended. American ship captain Henry Holmes, who made a number of trips to Japan prior to its opening to the West, noted in his journal, "They (the Japanese) will surprise the world!"

And surprise the world they have—in ways that have ranged from marvelous to shocking.

The first Westerners of record to visit Japan arrived by accident in 1543, having been blown off course by the

8

winds of a typhoon.

These Westerners, Portuguese traders who were passengers on a Chinese junk, introduced guns, tobacco and venereal disease to the Japanese. The next foreign visitor of note was a Jesuit priest named Francisco Xavier who arrived from the Portuguese settlement of Macau in 1549 determined to introduce the Japanese to Christianity.

Over the next several decades other missionaries and foreign traders by the hundreds descended upon Japan, eager to win minds or make fortunes.

The Japanese were unlike any people previously encountered by the globe-circling Europeans of the 16th century. They were roughly divided into two large classes— an elite sword-wearing warrior class, and common people. Their social system was based on vertical ranking within a military dictatorship headed by shoguns, and a highly sophisticated, rigidly enforced etiquette that governed all inter-personal relationships.

Male members of the warrior class, which made up about ten percent of the population, were fierce fighters who tended to be aggressive and arrogant. The mass of common people were characteristically polite, kind, generous, hospitable, trustworthy and diligent.

Most of the common people were rice and vegetable farmers. Others were fishermen, craftsmen and merchants. Members of the warrior class administered the laws of the country for the shogunate government.

This well-defined Japanese way of life, already more than a thousand years old at the beginning of the 16th century, was an elaborately refined combination of Shinto, Buddhist, Confucian and Daoist precepts that the Imperial Court, the Shogun's Court and the warrior class had molded into a unique culture which distinguished the Japanese from all other Asians, and especially made them different from Westerners.

These cultural differences intrigued and frustrated the first foreigners to arrive in Japan, many of whom spent a great deal of time trying to figure out why the Japanese thought and behaved the way they did. No one solved the enigma although a great deal of insight into Japanese behavior was gained in the attempt.

In the 1630s, fearing outside interference and eventual colonization attempts, Japan's feudal rulers expelled all foreign residents and closed the country to all except for one small Dutch trading post which was moved to a miniscule man-made islet in Nagasaki harbor. This isolated Dutch outpost was allowed one trade-ship visit per year. All other travel to and from the country was strictly prohibited and the penalty for contravening the law was death.

This ban remained in force until the 1850s when the U.S. sent a fleet of warships into Tokyo Bay to pry the country open, at the behest of American whalers, trading companies, and others who wanted to preempt Russia, England and other countries from gaining an advantage over the United States. In the years that followed, a flood of foreigners poured into Japan, some of them invited as technicians and teachers by the Meiji government that replaced the shogurtate, and others seeking the usual business profits and religious converts.

Over the next one hundred years Japan was studied, analyzed and dissected by thousands of foreign residents trying to understand the culture and devise ways of dealing effectively with the Japanese. Some of these early "old Japan hands" produced memorable books about the character and customs of the Japanese that are still read today.

Japan's miraculous recovery from the devastation of

World War II and its rapid climb to world power status resulted in massive new efforts to describe and explain the attitudes and behavior of the Japanese to the rest of the world—and in particular to explain why and how the Japanese were able to achieve extraordinary economic success in such a short period of time.

While most of the special traits and talents of the Japanese have now been accurately described by foreign businessmen, writers and scholars, no one has yet explained where these special traits and talents came from and how they became an integral part of Japanese culture.

I believe the answer to this puzzle lies in the special acculturation and training techniques called *shikata* (she-kah-tah)—or *kata* (kah-tah) when used in compound terms—developed and used by the Japanese over the centuries. This book looks at the origin, nature, use and influence of the kata factor in Japanese life.

I am greatly indebted to Dan Nakatsu, who spent many years in Japan as an airline and advertising executive, for encouraging me to focus on the kata factor in Japanese culture, and to old Japan hands Ken Butler, William K. Nichoson, Davis Barrager, Joseph P. Schmelzeis, Jr.—and several others who prefer not to be named—for reading the first draft of this book and making many suggestions for its improvement.

Boye Lafayette De Mente

1

THE KATA FACTOR
JAPAN'S TRADITIONAL SECRET WEAPON

Shikata (she-kah-tah) was traditionally one of the most used and most important words in the Japanese language. It means "way of doing things," with special emphasis on the form and order of the process. The root meaning of shi is a combination of "support" and "serve" in the sense of an inferior supporting and serving a superior. Kata, by itself, is usually translated as "form."

Some of the more common uses of kata included *yomi kata* (yoe-me kah-tah) or "way of reading;" *tabekata* (tah-bay kah-tah)—"way of eating;" *kaki kata* (kah-kee kah-tah) - "way of writing;" *kangaekata* (kahn-guy kah-tah)—"way of thinking;" *iki kata* (ee-kee kah-tah)—"way of living." There were dozens of other kata. In fact, there was hardly an area of Japanese thought or behavior that was not directly influenced by one or more kata.

When used in the Japanese context the shikata concept included more than just the mechanical process of doing something. It also incorporated the physical and spiritual laws of the cosmos. It referred to the way things are supposed to be done, both the form and the order, as a means of expressing and maintaining harmony in society and the universe.

The absence of shikata was virtually unthinkable to the Japanese, for that referred to an unreal world, without order or form. On an everyday level, when the Japanese were faced with something that cannot be changed or controlled (or for some reason they don't want to make the

12

necessary effort), they say, *Shikata ga nai* ("There is no way")—meaning it is utterly hopeless and therefore makes no sense even to try.

Early in their history the Japanese developed the belief that form had a reality of its own, and that it often took precedence over substance. They also believed that anything could be accomplished if the right kata was mentally and physically practiced long enough.

"Japan has no genuine philosophy as such, only form/' says Kazuo Matsumura, assistant professor of Japanese mythology at the Oyasato Institute at Tenri University in Nara. He adds, however, that most older Japanese today are ignorant of the roots of much of their kata-ized behavior.

The sum total of all the kata in Japanese life has traditionally been referred to as "The Japanese Way." It was the existence of this very conspicuous "way" that provided the Japanese with some of their most enviable as well as their most negative attributes, and distinguished them from other nationalities.

Most of Japan's numerous kata had been well established for centuries. Over the generations the kata not only became institutionalized they also became ritualized and sanctified. Doing things the right way was often more important than doing the right things!

Eventually, the proper observance of kata was equated with morality. One was either "in" kata—*kata ni hamaru* (kah-tah nee hah-mah-rue)—or "out" of kata—*kata ni hamaranai* (kah-tah nee hah-mah-rah-nigh). Being "out of kata" was a sin against society, and in form-conscious Japan could be fatal. Ethics gave way to styles; principles gave way to policies.

Just as there was only one acceptable way to perform all the various actions of life in pre-industrial Japan, from using chopsticks to wrapping a package, there was naturally only one right way of thinking—the "Japanese" way.

Cultural conditioning based on the kata system made the Japanese extremely sensitive to any thought, manner or action that did not conform perfectly to the appropriate kata. In formal as well as many daily situations every action was either right or wrong, natural or unnatural. There were no shades of gray that accommodated individualistic thought, preferences or idiosyncrasies.

To the Japanese there was an inner order (the individual heart) and a natural order (the cosmos), and these two were linked together by form—by kata. It was kata that linked the individual and society. If one did not follow the correct form, he was out of harmony with both his fellow man and nature. The challenge facing man was to know his own *honshin* (hone-sheen), "true" or "right heart," then learn and follow the kata that would keep one in sync with society and the cosmos.

MENTAL TRAINING

Zen priests have been teaching the Japanese since the 13th century that mental training is just as important, if not more so, than physical training in the achieving of harmony and the mastery of any skill. For young men in feudal Japan's samurai families this early mental teaching combined aesthetics with the more mundane skills of the world, particularly sword-fighting, which was frequently the final test in one's education—the inept pupil sometimes forfeiting his life.

The ultimate goal in traditional Japanese education among the samurai and professional classes was for the pupil to become one with the object of his training. The goal of the swordsman was to merge his consciousness with his sword; the painter with his brush; the potter with his clay; the garden designer with the materials of the garden. Once this was achieved, as the theory goes, the doing of a thing perfectly was as easy as thinking it.

Over the centuries each skill or profession making up the Japanese way of living was reduced to its basic elements. The elements were identified and labeled according to their order and the role they played in making up the whole. The learning of everyday behavior, proper etiquette, work skills and professions became a codified process of first learning the basic parts then developing skill in accomplishing the necessary actions in the prescribed order and manner.

Lifelong conditioning in this intricate, finely meshed web of rules and forms made it second nature for the Japanese to expect that every situation would have its exact process and form. When they were confronted with a situation that did not have its own kata they were either incapable of action or took action that was often the opposite of commonsense—and sometimes violent.

The significant difference between the Japanese Way and the customs that developed in most other societies was that the Japanese kata-ized their whole existence. Practically nothing was left to chance or personal inclinations. The kata factor was applied to everything—down to the arrangement of food on a tray. Further, the Japanese goal was not just the minimum acceptable standard of behavior, action or work...it was absolute perfection.

While few Japanese actually achieved total perfection in their behavior or pursuits, a very large percentage of the population certainly achieved a level of competence in the culture that starkly distinguished them from other national groups. And, as was graphically demonstrated in the latter half of the 20th century, gave them a number of real advantages in competing with the outside world.

THE SHIKATA OF HARMONY

The hallmark of Japan's kata-ized culture from earliest times has been the promotion and maintenance of *iva* (wah) or harmony. Personal behavior as well as all relationships, private and public, were based on strictly controlled harmony in the proper inferior-superior context of Japanese society.

This religious striving for harmony often went to the extreme and resulted in many laws and customs that were inhuman, such as collective guilt when only a single individual was at fault. Part: of the rationale for this harmony-based system can be traced to the political policies espoused by Prince Shotoku who served as regent to Empress Suiko in the 7th century and codified the idealized virtues of the Japanese in the country's first "constitution."

Prince Shotoku's constitution consisted of seventeen articles that provided the framework within which the country's unique culture was to develop thereafter. The first of these articles made harmony the foundation for all of the others. Prince Shotoku said that harmony consisted of not making polarized distinctions, and added that if a distinction could be made between good and bad, then harmony did not exist.

The prince was also well aware that envy destroys harmony. In another of his seventeen commandments he proclaimed:

"...If we envy other men, other men will envy us too. Evil derived from envy knows no end; thus people tend not to rejoice in superior wisdom. If you have superior talent you

16

will be the object of envy." The 17th and final commandment in Prince Shotoku's constitution was: "You must never decide great matters on your own. You must always discuss them with all kinds of people."

This effort to eliminate envy, prohibit individualism and suppress talent became a vital theme in Japanese culture. Jochi (Sophia) University linguist/historian Shoichi Watanabe characterizes the government policy of the whole Tokugawa period (1603-1868) as "eschew envy; hate ability; revere the past."

During the Tokugawa period [1603-1857] the shogunate passed numerous laws which prevented the development of commerce, the spread of new ideas and any rise in the standard of living—all in an effort to prevent changes in lifestyles and the appearance of such factors as envy and individual competition. One of the Tokugawa shoguns decreed: "You must never invent anything new!"

Jochi's Professor Watanabe has advanced the theory that the best way to discern and describe the traditional wa-oriented character of the Japanese is to compare them to peasant-farmers, locked in time and place, on a finite piece of soil from which they gain their livelihood. He says that a key part of the mentality that developed from this intimate relationship with land was a compulsion for harmony, since the survival of each village literally depended upon the strict observance of mutual concern and cooperation to build and maintain the complex irrigation systems needed to grow rice.

This "village mentality" continues to prevail in Japan in the form of groups and factions in business, politics, education and elsewhere. The Japanese still tend to regard any threat to the harmony of their immediate group, to their company or the country, as a matter of life and death

17

and to do whatever is necessary to protect and maintain wa.

Professor Watanabe concluded that respect for harmony is so strong in Japan that it continues to weed out most of the more competent, maverick-type individuals, frequently resulting in inferior leaders reaching the summit of the seniority system in all areas of Japanese life.

Examples of this syndrome are so commonplace in Japan that ordinarily they are taken for granted. Exceptions are growing, however, particularly in the political arena, where efforts to find and place acceptable prime ministers and other top officials has degenerated into a farce that the news media and people at large no longer accept without question.

A key factor in the Japanese culture of harmony is an attitude described by the word *amae* (ah-mah-eh), which means something like "indulgent love," and is the kind of love ideally found between infant and mother. The infant is utterly dependent on the mother and must totally trust the mother to do what is right and best for it. Likewise, the infant can indulge in the mother's forgiveness even when it is behaving badly.

Unquestioned "indulgent love" is, of course, known outside of Japan, but in the West its application is generally limited to infants and very young children. In Japan, however, it became one of the foundations for all relationships throughout life.

Traditional Japanese society incorporated the amae concept within specifically categorized and defined life-roles called *bun* (boon), which determined obligations and lifestyle within the individual categories. There was a bun— and kata—for carpenters, for merchants, for samurai, for students—even for professional gangsters.

18

These life-role bun provided strict guidelines for the prescribed relationship between children and parents, between younger and older siblings, between workers and their superiors, between samurai warriors and their lords, between the nation as a whole and the emperor. All of these relationships in turn had their own kata-ized behavioral guides.

The proper functioning of bun was based on every person knowing his place in life and keeping it according to the prescribed form, all the while demonstrating honesty, integrity, goodwill, trust, confidence and selflessness. Of course, the system seldom functioned fully, but the mass effort of the Japanese to live up to the expectations of their own kata-ized bun was one of the primary factors that shaped their character—and contributed to some early foreign residents remarking that living in Japan was like being in a kind of well-ordered paradise.

There were also other cultural factors designed to encourage or compel the Japanese to follow the kata-ized modes of behavior required by the bun roles of each individual. The most important of these concepts was expressed in the term *giri* (ghee-ree), which means "obligations." There were specific obligations that each person had to others—to teachers, employers, lords and so on. These obligations were spelled out in detail, and failure to fulfill them was a serious matter. Ostracization and banishment were some of the lighter punishments for the worst transgressions.

The immediate social sanction used to enforce strict obedience to the life obligations of the Japanese was shame, which was sometimes so intense and overpowering that the only acceptable recourse was suicide. One of the results of this system was that the Japanese became intensely sensitive to the threat of shame, highly suspicious of the motives of others, and correspondingly conditioned to seek revenge when they felt they had been wronged.

Both giri and shame are still very much alive in present-day Japan. One also constantly hears references to obligations that someone must fulfill because of his role in life—often much to his chagrin. These include obligatory gifts, attendance at weddings and funerals, catering to superiors, etc. Taking revenge, usually in subtle, behind-the-scene ways, remains a common preoccupation.

Japanese still strive to put and keep all of their relationships, personal as well as business, on an amae-impregnated role/rank basis. This is the factor that is at play when they go to such lengths and put so much stock in developing close, intimate relationships with foreigners before doing business with them. Most Japanese are unable to feel comfortable in anything but a clearly defined socially ranked relationship "made safe" by the belief that they can expect indulgence from the other party when accidently or purposely breaking some of the rules of the relationship.

Many Japanese, in all areas of business and government, attribute the country's Phoenix-like recovery from the destruction of World War II to the principle of kata-ized wa that underpins their culture. They hold that it was harmonious relations between labor and management, between business and the government and between individuals that made it possible for the people to work together with a single-minded determination that created the so-called economic miracle.

Other commentators, particularly long-term foreign

residents who have become bilingual and bicultural, say that the still powerful shame syndrome, along with a consuming pride, were the primary motivating factors that drove the Japanese in their superhuman efforts to not only rebuild their country but to become one of the world's leading economic powers.

Social harmony, based on following proper etiquette kata in daily behavior (under the threat of being ostracized) remains the guiding principle in all Japanese relations, whether personal, business or political. The wa concept pervades the culture. It appears as wall art in the form of calligraphy. It is a key part of such common words as peace (heiwa), peaceful resolution (wa kai), and peaceful concord (wa go). The original name of the country, Yamato, is written with the characters for "Great Harmony" (Dai Wa). The deeply entrenched concept of "Japanese spirit," Yamato damashii, is also read as wa kon when the character for "great" is dropped.

Some Japanese who attribute the country's success to the spirit of wa claim it is contained in their genes. This, of course, is nonsense, as is evidenced by the hundreds of thousands of Japanese-Americans who are fully assimilated into American culture and, as American expatriate businessman Joe Schmelzeis Jr. once remarked, "Speak with their mouths, not their bellies."

Japan marketing guru George Fields also disagreed with this gene theory. He said wa in Japan today is better described in business terms, as "corporate spirit, unity of employees, and the consumer always comes last." He added that much of the wa that survives in Japan results from government pressure and guidance.

Examples of Japanese style wa abound. More candid government officials and company executives readily admit that *dango* (dahn-go) or "bid rigging," is common in Japan, but to them it is just wa at work. Until foreigners began complaining about the practice it was not considered an ethical issue. The Japanese involved were perplexed and irritated that foreigners made an issue of it, but a few isolated complaints from outsiders are not enough to eliminate a culturally entrenched kata that serves the Japanese establishment so well.

The original goal of wa was social harmony and political control. Now, as George Fields noted, its primary role is to contribute to economic success on a corporate, industry and national level.

In practice, the Japanese government's policy of promoting harmony sometimes clashes with the interests of individual companies, and corporate managers go along with it grudgingly if at all. On a company level, adherence to the principles of wa is usually confined to the company itself and to any closely affiliated companies. Sub-contract firms are generally treated as expendable. Other outside firms are regarded as competitors and adversaries.

A not surprising characteristic of the Japanese that derives from their emphasis on correct form and harmony is their tendency to avoid doing things altogether if they are uncertain about how to do them. This trait is part of the reason the Japanese are often reluctant to set any precedent and habitually wait for someone else or some other company to take the lead. This attitude is often one of the main barriers foreign companies face in attempting to do business in Japan.

THE FEELING OF RIGHTNESS

Born and raised in a cultural environment that was

the result of centuries of conditioning in the art of living Japanese style and in the use of arts and crafts that were products of rigidly controlled kata, each Japanese naturally developed a sixth sense that told him when things were "right"—that is, when they were designed, made, assembled, packaged or whatever in accordance with Japanese concepts of aesthetics, appropriate materials, form, feel, purpose and method of use.

Over the centuries these standards became higher and higher, ultimately demanding that even the most commonplace product be a masterpiece of crafts-manship and all service be performed with consummate, stylized skill.

Japanese naturally became so sensitive to the Tightness or correctness of any service or product, measured by absolute Japanese standards, that they knew almost instinctively when something did riot measure up to these standards. This traditional characteristic reaction made them among the most discriminating people in the world, and often the quickest to pass judgment.

Japan's early reputation for cheap, shoddy products, which endured from 1870 until the 1960s, was not of their own doing, and undeserved. When the country was opened to the West in the 1860s foreign importers flocked in, bringing with them samples of Western products they wanted copied at the lowest possible prices. These first foreign importers and those who followed them determined the quality of most of Japan's exports until the Japanese became strong enough to escape from their influence nearly one hundred years later. Japan-made products have been superior in quality since the 1960s.

While social and economic changes in Japan have greatly diluted kata-ized conditioning in the traditional culture and, subsequently, the discriminating abilities of Japanese born after 1945, the Japanese as a group are still among the most critical people in the world. Their culturally produced emphasis on aesthetic excellence, quality and propriety remains one of their primary strengths. It gave them an edge in designing, manufacturing and packaging products, as well as in promoting and selling them. It also made them very demanding customers.

This aspect of modern Japanese culture is so prominent that Japanologist-linguist Ken Butler remarked that generally the Japanese are innately imbued with the attitudes and skills that make good businessmen.

THE UNIQUENESS FACTOR

Long centuries of living within the kata-ized Japanese way and never seeing, much less experiencing, any other way of daily life naturally led the Japanese to become acutely sensitive to any deviation from their way of doing things. This factor contributed significantly to their developing especially strong feelings of being unique in the world—feelings that persist today and influence their personal behavior toward non-Japanese, business relations with foreign companies, and government policy in international affairs.

These differences were so conspicuous that one veteran observer, paraphrasing an earlier commentator, said jokingly: "The Japanese are so unique that it is uniquely impossible to describe their uniqueness."

Unfortunately Japanese feelings of uniqueness are often expressed in a very negative manner. Among other things, it makes it very difficult, or impossible, for un-Westernized Japanese to relate to non-Japanese. Even other Japanese who

24

become partially de-Japanized by spending time abroad are treated, in varying degrees, as outcasts in their own society after they return home.

School children who have spent time abroad and lost some of their Japaneseness are harassed by other students and in many cases even their teachers. (In recent years, special schools have been built to help re-acculturate such children so that they are better able to re-enter Japanese society.) Businessmen who have picked up foreign attitudes and mannerisms while serving their companies on overseas assignments often find that they are no longer fully accepted by their own co-workers or management when they return home.

In earlier decades most major Japanese companies tended to follow a policy of not hiring non-Japanese employees within Japan, including ethnic Korean and Chinese residents who were born and raised in Japan, are citizens and are virtually indistinguishable from ethnic Japanese. The rationale for this policy was that non-Japanese did not, and cannot, fit into the Japanese system because they are not Japanese.

This discrimination was also regularly applied to Japan's minority population of "untouchables" whose only difference is that they are descendants of Japanese who were involved in the slaughter of animals and worked with animal hides during the country's Buddhist dominated period. Larger Japanese firms were known to buy lists of names and addresses of families in this group in order to avoid inadvertently hiring one—there being no other way to distinguish them from other Japanese.

Japanese feelings of uniqueness was frequently taken to even further extremes, making them appear foolish. Attempting to justify import barriers against foreign-made ski equipment by claiming that snow in Japan is different from snow in other countries (so the equipment won't work in Japan) is just one example. (The fact that they were exporting Japanese-made skis did not have any effect on the reasoning of the trade associations involved.)

In the past, Japanese have also used their perceived uniqueness to justify all kinds of discrimination against both foreign nationals and products at every level of Japanese society, an attitude that has surfaced as part of their national policy. This attitude and behavior was directly opposed to attempts to internationalize the country, and thwarted many of the efforts on both the government and private level to bring Japan into the world family.

Racial, cultural, sexual and age discrimination by Japanese companies were not limited to their domestic practices. Some took the same mind-set with them over-seas, where they have encountered serious repercussions from their refusal to hire blacks and sometimes whites as well.

KATA COMES FIRST

The Japanese were traditionally conditioned to get their pleasure from conforming to kata, from doing things in the prescribed manner. One of the effects of this conditioning was to make the Japanese process-oriented instead of result-oriented. Westerners are fond of saying, "I don't care how you do it, just get it done." Japanese tend to say, "Don't do it unless you can do it right (the right way)."

Japanese are happiest when they improve on a process, says management guru Masaru Chio. "They are perfectionists. The slightest flaw in anything attracts their attention and they cannot rest until it is eliminated/' he added.

Because of this attitude there is a strong tendency for the Japanese to try to improve on any job they undertake, particularly when using technology or copying products imported from abroad. They often seem to spend as much or more time on refining processes as they do on producing results. But once refinements have been made, their performance often shoots upward.

Not surprisingly, the traditional Japanese standard when measuring or evaluating individuals was attitude first, effort second, and results third. In sports and other activities, participants were honored and rewarded in recognition of their attitude, spirit and effort as well as their victories.

Proper observance of every traditional kata in today's Japan is no longer a life and death issue and some kata have nearly disappeared. However, others are still of vital importance, coloring and often controlling the thoughts and actions of virtually all adult Japanese in many areas of their lives.

Japanese kata for negotiating, for example, play a vital role not only in business, but in international relations as well. Kinhide Mushako ji, formerly professor of international relations at Sophia University in Tokyo, described the Japanese kata of diplomacy and negotiating as the art of *awase* (ah-wah-say) or "adjustment," while Westerners follow an *erabi* (aye-rah-bee) or "choice" style.

In other words, the Japanese negotiate by adjusting or adapting to differences, while Westerners negotiate by selecting specific options. The Japanese take a broad, flexible approach. Westerners tend to take a more narrow, highly defined approach. The Japanese seek nonspecific generalities that take into account all the shades in between specifics. Westerners demand a logical structure made up of specific concepts and their opposites.

Japanese society lives by the kata of adjustment, seemingly with few hard and fast ethics or clear-cut moral rules of the type found in Western cultures. It is soft and flexible and can be readily manipulated by self-seeking and aggressive individuals and groups within the society. Christianized societies, on the other hand, attempt to live by principles embodying hard, inflexible rules. It should not be surprising that meetings between Japanese and Westerners often result in misunderstandings and friction.

THE COMING OF FOREIGNERS

Because of the intense cultural conditioning undergone by all Japanese during the feudal age, any deviation from "correct" thought and form was a serious moral and ethical transgression. Behaving in any way other than "the Japanese way" was unthinkable for the average person. Thus, when foreigners who behaved in a vastly different manner began showing up in Japan the Japanese were shocked at their lack of kata and crude etiquette. To the Japanese the foreigners looked, behaved and smelled like "hairy barbarians" with whom they had almost nothing in common.

Still today the Japanese are extraordinarily sensitive to the appearance, attitudes and behavior of foreigners. Because of the exclusivity of Japanese culture, some Japanese are unable to accept foreigners as equals, and tend to be comfortable with them only when they are in Japan as temporary visitors. As long as foreigners can be treated as guests, the Japanese are able to exempt them from the demands of Japanese culture, and can extend extraordinary courtesies and privileges to them.

Non-guest foreigners in Japan may encounter the cultural dichotomy that prevents some Japanese from fully accepting them on any basis except as temporary visitors. Foreigners in Japan must therefore continuously be aware that as tolerant and hospitable as their Japanese hosts are to short-term visitors, who are not expected to know or practice their kata-ized etiquette, they are still emotionally affected when anyone, foreigners included, behaves "incorrectly."

Over and above this sensitivity, the Japanese are prone to regard normal "give-and-take" Western behavior as arrogant, often inhuman and typically ill-mannered, while Japanese behavior often appears insincere, devious and dishonest to Westerners once they get beyond the famous facade of Japanese courtesy. Intimate knowledge of the kata factor helps to bridge this cultural chasm by sensitizing the "visiting" foreigner to the need to observe "proper" behavior, and to avoid situations in which non-conformity would seriously jeopardize the goals at hand.

It is especially important for foreign businessmen, politicians and diplomats dealing with the Japanese to become familiar with Japan's kata-ized etiquette system and their special sensitivities in order to avoid creating unnecessary ill will.

Specific kata and how they impact on all inter-personal relationships with the Japanese, along with strategies for dealing with them, are discussed in some detail in the following chapters.

2
THE KATA-IZATION OF JAPAN

THE WAY OF THE GODS

The origins of Japan's extraordinary kata can be traced to a number of historical influences, beginning with the native religion of Shintoism, generally translated as "The Way of the Gods" and continuing with the introduction of the irrigation method of rice farming, and the importation of Buddhism, Confucianism, the ideographic writing system and various other cultural artifacts from China.

Shintoism is an animistic belief based on cosmic harmony among gods, spirits, people and the physical world of nature. It is the indirect, but culturally pervasive, source, of many of the attitudes and customs that distinguish the Japanese from all other people. It was apparently the influence of Shintoism that led the Japanese to refer to themselves as the people of Wa, attesting to a very early commitment by the Japanese to the principle of harmony as the foundation for their society.

The first emperors of Japan combined the functions of religious and secular leaders, serving as high priests as well as sovereigns. The emperors and their courts were thus as much concerned with form as with essence. An overriding principle, adopted from Confucianism, was harmony between heaven and earth, and between rulers and the ruled.

This led to the development of a highly controlled

30

behavior designed to express subservience and respect toward superior beings. The stylized ceremonies associated with worship were thus infused into the conduct of daily affairs.

Japanese affinity for formalizing, institutionalizing and ritualizing procedures and processes may not have actually originated in Shintoism but this characteristic Japanese behavior was surely nurtured by the pervasive religious practices that marked life in early Japan. Conducting precise religious rituals dozens of times throughout each year was a major aspect of Japanese life from the dawn of their history, and in each family at least one member was expected to be versed in these rites.

Whatever the origin of the wa concept, it was to become one of the main threads in the cultural fabric of Japan, influencing its form, its texture, its color and its spirit.

THE WAY OF WET-RICE FARMING

Japanese social anthropologists believe that the introduction of irrigated wet-rice farming into Japan from China sometime between 1,000 and 300 B.C. had an especially profound effect on the country's social system and subsequently the character and behavior of the Japanese. Many historians claim that the lifestyle that emerged with wet-rice farming in such a limited land area imbued the Japanese with an extraordinary degree of patience, perseverance, diligence,* cooperativeness and group dependence because this kind of farming required very elaborate irrigation systems that could not easily be built and maintained—or protected from marauders—by single families.

Among the most conspicuous Japanese traits said to have been fostered by wet-rice farming was the acceptance of discipline and regimentation. The individual who did not conform was quickly ostracized to protect and sustain the group. The process of rice farming was prescribed down to the last detail. Any deviation angered not only one's family, friends and neighbors, but the gods as well. The whole economic base of the country therefore became one giant rice-raising kata that made group behavior, cooperation, self-sacrifice and harmony mandatory.

Also very early in Japan's history, probably sometime before 300 A.D., the concept of *kochi komin* (koe-chee koe-meen), in which the land and the people belonged to the emperor and the people had no ultimate right to own private property or to be independent, was imported from China. This helped to set the stage for virtually absolute control of the people by the state and the gradual development of many of the other cultural traits that were to distinguish the Japanese down to modern times.

THE COUNTRY OF WA

Prior to A.D. 300, Japanese society consisted of relatively independent family clans that exercised domain in their own small areas. Around A.D. 300, one of these clans became paramount in the area now known as Kara Prefecture (a short distance from Kyoto and Osaka) and established itself as the Yamato Court, claiming sovereignty over the entire country. Later historians labeled the first leader of the Yamato Court as Jimmu Tenno or Emperor Jimmu.

Succeeding emperors continued the process of unifying the country, which came to be known as *Yamato* (Yah-mah-toe) after the founding clan. Yamato is another reading for the word wa or harmony, once again attesting to an early fundamental commitment by the Japanese to the concept of a harmonious society.

Following the ascendancy of Japan's Yamato Court to power, however, several military expeditions were launched against Korea—an early sign that harmony in the Japanese context was primarily designed to shape and channel Japanese behavior for internal purposes and did not specifically apply to their relationships with outsiders.

These Japanese raids on Korea resulted in a mass influx of Chinese-Korean cultural influences into Japan, mostly through Korean prisoners and immigrants, and later Chinese scholars and priests. Thereafter, Korea and China were to play leading roles in the development of both culture and kata in Japan.

From around A.D. 550 two-way travel and trade between Japan, Korea and China became quite common. Religious scholars in particular served as conduits for importing Chinese culture into the islands. The ritualized ceremonies of China's Imperial Court and the sophisticated etiquette that China's ministers and mandarins had developed over a period of more than 3,000 years were gradually assimilated into Japan's already highly structured Imperial system.

Decorum and language appropriate for addressing the god-like emperor of Japan became exquisitely stylized and then codified. Every movement of the body, every stance, even the tone of the voice, was precisely established. An only slightly less lofty level of etiquette was required for other members of the Imperial Court.

As time passed a system of clan fiefs and clan lords became the paramount political and social structure in Japan. These clan lords set up their own governments, patterning them after the Imperial Court in form as well as ritualistic behavior. Court etiquette was thus brought to elite families throughout the country, further strengthening the custom of ritualizing all training and learning.

THE MOTHER KATA

When Japan first began intercourse with Korea and China the Japanese had no system of writing. Around the middle of the 3rd century a scholar named Wani brought several volumes of the *Analects of Confucius* and a textbook for studying the Chinese writing system to Japan from Korea, but very little came of this incident. By the early 4th century, however, the Imperial Court of Japan was employing Koreans who had migrated to Japan to serve as official recorders using the Chinese way of writing, which the Japanese called *Kan-Ji* (Kahn-Jee), or "Chinese Letters."

Kan-Ji had gradually evolved in China over a period of a thousand years or so, beginning as rather straightforward "pictures" of the things and ideas they represented. Little by little, these pictures were stylized to make them more consistent in shape and size and therefore easier to draw in large numbers on small sheets or scrolls of paper, as well as more aesthetically attractive. By the time the "characters" arrived in Japan they were the world's most sophisticated system of writing.

Over the next hundred or so years the descendants of these Korean scribes gradually transcribed most of the Japanese language into Kan-Ji. In this extraordinary grafting process they used the Japanese pronunciation when the original meaning of the Chinese ideograms and the Japanese words were the same, and maintained the Chinese pronunciation when they were not.

Since each Chinese character expressed a single idea it was necessary to make numerous adaptations and additions to the system in order to express complete thoughts in Japanese. One of these adaptations was to use Chinese characters that had the same sound as Japanese syllables or words regardless of the original meaning of the Chinese ideograms. Another was to use a phonetic script to add the proper Japanese word endings to the base Chinese characters.

Memorizing and learning how to read and write thousands of complicated Chinese characters, with their multiple pronunciations, was a challenge of immense proportions and beyond the means of most Japanese who lacked the time and motivation.

In keeping with Confucian principles of separating the sexes, females were forbidden to study the imported Chinese ideograms. Because of this Imperial edict, ladies of the Imperial Court and the aristocracy resorted to using the word-ending phonetic script, and subsequently played a key role in developing it into a simple shorthand system of writing the entire language phonetically.

This new phonetic syllabary system developed by upper-class women became known as *onna-te* (own-nah tay) or "women's hand," since it was used almost exclusively by women for private communication and the writing of poetry, diaries and, later, novels. This is the writing system now known as *hira-gana* (hee-rah-gah-nah) or "flat letters."

In a further effort to simplify the writing of the language a totally separate phonetic system, derived from parts of the multi-stroke Chinese characters, was developed by scholars in the 9th and 10th centuries. This second phonetic system became known as *kata-kana* (kah-tah-kah-nah) or "incomplete letters"—and is the one now used in Japan for writing the thousands of foreign words that have been absorbed into the language.

Despite the creation of two phonetic writing systems, the difficult Kan-Ji remained the writing system of the Imperial Court, the agencies of the government, the priesthood and the male members of the upper classes for century after century, eventually becoming one of the primary crucibles of Japanese culture and the Japanese we know today.

Each Kan-Ji was made up of one to a dozen or more conjoining strokes. The order in which each stroke was to be executed was carefully prescribed and no deviation was allowed. Among Japan's upper class, boys began the long process of learning how to read and write Kan-Ji from about the age of five, spending a number of hours each day for the next several years practicing the prescribed kaki-kata or "way of writing."

Since the Chinese ideographs depicted actual things and concepts, they communicated more than just sounds as per our familiar ABCs. Using them as a system of communicating and recording information and concepts was therefore much more of a personal experience, with far deeper and stronger psychological content than words spelled with phonetic letters. In a recent experiment where various strokes were combined to create non-existent Kan-Ji, Japanese respondents frequently argued with each other over the "correct" meanings of the "characters."

The mental concentration and kata-ized mechanical

36

effort required to memorize and write thousands of Kan-Ji correctly had a fundamental effect on the psychological and physical development of all educated Japanese males. It ingrained in them patience and diligence, enhanced manual dexterity well beyond the norm, and prepared them for a lifestyle in which form and order were paramount.

Learning how to draw the Kan-Ji characters also imbued educated Japanese with a highly developed sense of harmony, form and style that combined to give them a deep understanding and appreciation of aesthetics, making each of them an artist of no little skill.

In addition to making the Japanese good at doing small, complicated things with their hands and enhancing their sensitivity to forms and designs, training in writing Kan-Ji also conditioned the Japanese to be patient and to persevere in their goals. The long-term practice of Kan-Ji thus became a mold that shaped the Japanese physically, emotionally and intellectually, homogenizing them and binding them to their culture.

Learning Kan-Ji during Japan's long feudal age did not end with mastering their pronunciations, meanings and correct stroke order. Every student of the art was also required to become adept at drawing the characters in a stylized manner known as *Sho-Do* (show-doe), "The Way of the Brush," or calligraphy in English.

When skill in writing the Kan-Ji ideograms was pursued beyond basic requirements, which many Japanese did, it became a fine art. The greatest calligraphers won lasting fame. In fact, skill in writing the ideograms became so important during the heyday of Japan's feudal age (A.D. 1192-1868) that how well one could write became a measure of his character and worthiness.

Midway during the period that the character and skill-building Kan-Ji writing system was being introduced into Japan, the Imperial government institutionalized the concept of a carefully prescribed harmony. Wa became the official policy of the government in A.D. 604 when Prince Shotoku named it as the foundation of all human relations in his famous "Seventeen Articles," which later historians were to call Japan's first constitution.

With wa firmly established as the essence of their social system the upper-class Japanese thereafter fashioned all of their social rules and institutions as well as their language to contribute to the cultural goal of harmony. No area or facet of Japanese life was untouched by this one overriding principle.

HANDICRAFTS AND ARTS

Along with the Chinese writing system the Japanese of this early age also imported virtually all the leading Chinese arts and crafts, with the master-apprentice teaching system, creating new cottage industries that eventually spread throughout the country. Once the Japanese learned the basics of these new arts and crafts, they began experimenting with the designs and production techniques, adapting them to suit their own tastes.

Learning the skills necessary to duplicate a Chinese handicraft or fine art took many years, however, and sometimes more than one lifetime. Boys, often as young as eight or nine, were apprenticed to skilled craftsmen and artists, sometimes for as many as thirty or even forty years, to master each craft or art. They in turn passed the skill on to their own apprentices.

Given their natural propensity for structuring and

formalizing everything, the earliest of these Japanese crafts-men and artists refined their specialized techniques into minutely detailed kata that covered not only physical actions but attitudes as well.

Every thought, every move, every nuance of the arts and crafts kata were established, and—just as in writing Kan-Ji—deviations were not tolerated. While this insured that the mastery of each craft would be passed on from generation to generation, in many cases it also prevented further experimentation and change—a factor that was eventually to contribute to the stagnation of Japanese culture during the final centuries of the feudal era.

In one sense the Japanese of feudal Japan were in training for nearly two thousand years for the op-portunities that were to be presented to them in 1945, when for the first time in their history, they gained much broader individual freedom and could engage freely in a more unrestrained and competitive market. It was only in such a free environment that they could fully utilize the extraordinary sensibilities and skills they had devel-oped over a period of nearly two millennia.

SHIKATA OF THE SAMURAI

By the beginning of the 12th century most of the authority of Japan's Imperial Court had been usurped by powerful provincial clan lords who maintained their own armies of warriors. In the 1180s, Yoritomo Minamoto, a leader of one of these warrior groups, defeated the other lords in a series of battles and emerged as the supreme power in the country.

Minamoto petitioned the reigning emperor for approval to set up a military government to administer the civil and military affairs of the country, and to use the title *Shogun* (Show-goon) or Generalissimo.[†] The emperor had little choice. Minamoto established his headquarters in Kamakura, far to the northeast of the Imperial capital of Kyoto (a one hour train-ride south of present-day Tokyo). He then confirmed the positions of the provincial clan lords who had fought on his side during the war and confiscated the lands of the losing lords, reassigning them to his allies.

The Kamakura period marked the beginning of the shogunate system of military government that was to prevail in Japan until 1868, nearly 700 years later, when the last shogun stepped down. Warriors of the shogunate and the clan lords were known as samurai, a derivative of the word meaning "to guard" or "guards." The profession of samurai soon became hereditary and reached new levels of development as a class of warrior families ranked at the top of the social system.

Over the generations, the samurai warriors developed their own "class" kata comprising a collective code of thought and conduct known as *Bushido* (Buu-she-doe) or "The Way of the Warrior/' which applied to all the members of their families. This code demanded absolute loyalty to the clan lord, extraordinary skill with the sword and other weapons of war on the part of male members of samurai families, plus adherence to the ritualized etiquette followed by the Imperial and clan courts.

Achieving the skills and commitment demanded by

[†] *Shogun is short for *Sei-i-hii Shogun* (Say-e-e-tie Show-guun) or Barbarian-Subduing Generalissimo, used centuries earlier in campaigns against the Caucasoid Ainu people who inhabited the northern regions of Japan when the racial groups which came to be known as the Japanese arrived on the scene.

Bushido required supreme dedication and effort. The discipline and techniques of Zen Buddhism, which was introduced into Japan from China during the 13th century, were quickly adopted by the samurai and became one of the primary vehicles for their physical as well as spiritual training.

Zen was a significant move away from the mystical and esoteric beliefs and practices of Shintoism and Buddhism. It was based on realism and practicality. Its goal was to help advocates discern between the real and the imaginary, and to achieve perfect harmony between the body and the mind through rigorous mental and physical discipline.

The goal of Zen followers in feudal Japan was to make all of the actions of life an expression of Zen—actions that could be perfected only through meditation to achieve harmony with the universe, followed by physical practice to teach the body the proper moves. Every adherent was to be an example of living Zen.

Zen practice was just as carefully codified as the making of a piece of pottery or proper behavior in greeting and conversing with a high-ranking superior. There was a prescribed way for the process from beginning to end. Meditation was the way to understanding the relationship between man and the world at large. Mental discipline was the key to controlling and directing the body. Endless physical practice in the desired skills was the third step in Zen training.

Training in Zen practices were ritualized, institutionalized and kata-ized like everything else in Japanese life. Zen priests were also hard taskmasters, demanding extraordinary endurance, perseverance and dedication from those wanting to sharpen their mental and physical skills as well as their awareness. Those who pursued Zen practices rigorously for many years often developed a kind of sixth sense that greatly expanded their ability to hear and understand and to "know" things that could not be seen.

The Zen-inspired kata training system of the samurai also further conditioned this elite class of Japanese to sacrifice their lives in the pursuit of perfection and order and the successful carrying out of their obligations to their masters— all traits that are still today associated with the Japanese in general.

Japan's many Zen temples are still thriving today and in fact experienced a wave of renewed interest in the 1970s, particularly among businessmen who rediscovered the advantages of using the traditional discipline and philosophy of Zen as a weapon in their competition with domestic as well as foreign business adversaries. Thousands of Japanese managers now spend part of their on-the-job training time in Zen temples, undergoing the rigorous discipline of meditation sessions to develop patience, perseverance, endurance and, they hope, cosmic wisdom.

During the long course of Japan's feudal age when the samurai class reigned supreme (1192-1868), much of the ethics, morality and manners of the samurai were gradually absorbed to a significant degree by the lower classes, particularly by the merchant class that rose during the last centuries of the shogunate dynasties from the mid-17th century on.

SHIKATA OF THE SWORD

The kata of martial arts epitomized the training and the lifestyle of the samurai class. Male members of samurai families spent years perfecting their physical and mental skills in the use of the sword. This dedication and training was carried to the point where the sword came to be regarded as semi-sacred and as representing the soul, spirit and pride of samurai warriors. Dropping a samurai's sword or mishandling it in any way brought many luckless Japanese a painful death at the hands of the sword owner.

Sword-making was constantly refined and im-proved until each weapon was a work of art that surpassed swords being made anywhere else in beauty, strength and cutting edge. Swordsmiths would spend months finding the right pieces of metal to blend, then weeks to months working on a single blade. Fashioning and honing the blade became a Shinto-based ritualistic process intended to imbue the finished sword with its own spirit.

The practicing of swordsmanship by all of the males in the samurai class was to have a profound influence on all Japanese and Japanese history from this time on. Training in the use of the sword began when the sons of samurai were three or four years old, and continued throughout their active lives as warriors.

Until the end of the feudalistic shogunate system in 1868, any samurai warrior was legally permitted to cut down, on the spot, any commoner guilty of breaking a law or behaving in a disrespectful manner. This was a great incentive for the Japanese mass to obey all laws and codes of etiquette.

During Japan's long feudal age only members of the samurai class were allowed to practice swordsmanship, which was known as *Ken-Do* or the "Way of the Sword" (usually written in Roman letters as "kendo"). Kendo schools were operated in all the clan fiefs as well as in larger cities and towns. During the early feudal centuries, solid wooden staffs instead of real swords were used in the training. Since a stout staff in the hands of a strong opponent can be as deadly as a steel sword, the training and exhibition bouts were very serious matters.

In addition to honing the sword-fighting skills of the samurai, training in kendo also emphasized the spiritual and moral responsibilities of warriors, along with the highly stylized manners that were the hallmark of the samurai class.

Following the establishment of the Tokugawa Shogunate in 1603, and the beginning of a long peaceful era, the injury and death toll from kendo training became unacceptable. The use of solid staffs gave way to flexible bamboo strips tied together. Protective gear that included helmets and face masks, torso guards and gauntlets was developed and routinely used—except in the case of grudge or revenge bouts when the contestants reverted to the traditional staffs, without protection.

When the shogunate system of government and the privileged samurai class were ended in 1868, kendo schools catering to common people soon sprang up. Officers of the Imperial Army of Japan were trained in the use of the sword up to 1945.

Following the introduction of democracy into Japan after the end of World War II the practice of kendo became an important means of developing character rather than martial prowess. Today kendo is a popular public school curriculum and is taught in many private kendo schools operated by masters of the art. It is also a significant part of the training of Japanese police.

The kata of kendo, codified hundreds of years ago, is still precisely followed in Japan's kendo schools. All of the moves and thrusts as well as the accompanying etiquette are minutely detailed. Boys begin training as early as the age of five or six. Training sessions are designed to instill courage, aggressiveness and an inexhaustible spirit.

Kendo and its kata make a significant contribution to the mental and physical training of large numbers of Japanese, further conditioning them in the etiquette and morality of the Japanese Way as well as strengthening will and spirit in their personal and business dealings.

THE RITUAL OF TEA

Perhaps no aspect of traditional Japanese culture is more representative of the role and importance of kata than the practice of the tea ceremony, or *Chanoyu* (chah-no-yuu). The custom of ceremonial tea-drinking was introduced into Japan from Korea and China in the 700s.

At first the custom was followed mainly by emperors, members of the Imperial Court and Buddhist priests. Priests would gather in front of a statue of Buddha and drink tea with all of the ritualistic formality of a holy sacrament. As the centuries passed, the ceremonial aspects faded, only to be revived during the Kamakura Perod (1185-1333). Juko Murata, tea master to Shogun Yoshimasa Ashikaga, is credited with turning the ceremony into an aesthetic ritual during the 1400s. The ceremony was further developed and codified by the famed Sen no Rikyu during the 1500s.

With Shogun Yoshimasa Ashikaga as a patron, the ritualistic drinking of tea quickly developed into a public ceremony that was regularly staged by numerous people. Tea houses abounded. The purpose of the ceremony was to develop and demonstrate one's aesthetic abilities and the ultimate in refined manners.

The kata of charioyu was minutely detailed, covering not only the place, dress, actions and state of mind but the weather as well. Staging a ceremony was not a casual skill. It was an art that required years of practice, and for many was a profession of the most exacting kind. Tea masters were among those honored as the great men of their times.

Practicing chanoyu was believed to develop refinement and character along with control of the body and the mind—all traits especially prized by the Japanese.

The tea ceremony remains a major cultural practice in present-day Japan. There are many "schools," hundreds of tea masters and thousands of specially built rooms where ceremonies are staged regularly. Hundreds of thousands of individuals, particularly successful older men and women, regularly conduct tea ceremonies for special friends as well as just for themselves alone.

Besides training and exercising aesthetic ability, tea ceremonies also teach Japan's highly refined etiquette, patience, endurance and precision. Practiced properly, a tea ceremony has a calming effect on the nerves and emotions, lowers blood-pressure and puts one in a peaceful mood.

The tea ceremony is not only an exercise in kata culture, it is also a kind of therapy that many Japanese utilize to rid themselves of the stress of the modern-day world, particularly the non-Japanese aspects of present-day society and business.

THE SHIKATA OF SUMO

Sumo (sue-moe), or Japanese style wrestling, dates back to well before the beginning of Japan's written history. It is an excellent example of kata because it is in fact a quin-

46

tessential Japanese activity—demonstrating in a very public way the Japanese emphasis on order and form, ceremony and ritual—and because it has survived virtually unchanged and is more popular and significant today than it was a thousand years ago.

Fans of sumo are well aware of its detailed kata, from the feeding and training of the wrestlers to their techniques in the ring. Every facet of the lives of sumo wrestlers is covered by kata, down to how the huge men manage to perform their conjugal duties as husbands.

Sumo began as an oracular ritual performed at Shinto shrines to ensure good harvests. Over the centuries it gradually became a spectator sport, at first still associated with shrines. Eventually local lords and bosses began sponsoring their own champions. Some bouts between the champions of competing lords were fights to the death.

The attractions of sumo are closely bound up in its conformity to ancient customs and ceremonies. The giant-sized loin cloths the wrestlers wear, their entry into the ring, the ceremonial toss of purifying salt, the repeated confrontations between wrestlers before they attack, the squatting of the winner at ring-side, and the final twirling of the bow at the day's end, all are part of the kata of sumo.

Sumo has some seventy precisely catalogued ways of attacking an opponent and either forcing him to touch the ground inside the ring, with anything other than his feet, or ejecting him from the ring. But only a dozen or so of the moves are commonly used. All of these precise moves are totally familiar to fans, and are commented on endlessly by sumo sportscasters covering the bouts for radio and television audiences.

Sumo became a nationally organized profession during the Tokugawa or Edo period (1603-1868). There are presently six tournaments a year, each lasting for fifteen days, meaning there are bouts for ninety of the three hundred and sixty five days of the year. Exhibition bouts are held in addition to the regularly scheduled tournaments, and in between tournaments fans may visit the different sumo *beya* (bay-yah) or "stables" to watch their favorites in training.

During the spring, summer, fall and winter tournaments the sumo stadiums are packed with loyal fans, while millions of others watch the daily bouts on television—all feeling a strong kinship for the kata of the sport and lavishing praise on wrestlers who excel in the various techniques.

THE SHIKATA OF POETRY

Writing poetry has been a popular pastime in Japan for more than a thousand years. The institutionalized custom may have been imported from China between the fourth and seventh centuries, but prior to this period Japan had professional oral historians along with storytellers and entertainers who often expressed their commentary in the form of poetry.

The introduction of the Kan-Ji writing system into Japan between the fourth and seventh centuries spurred the writing of Chinese style poetry but did not result in popularizing poetry-writing among the masses, however, because learning Kan-Ji was limited to upper-class males. Teachers were strictly prohibited from instructing even upper-class women in how to read and write the semi-sacred characters.

It was not until the eighth and nine centuries when a simplified phonetic writing system based on Kan-Ji was developed that women and others were allowed to learn how to write, resulting in a massive outpouring of literature. The new system provided an extraordinary impetus for the leisured court ladies of Kyoto to make the writing of poetry an important part of their lifestyle. Japan's first anthologies of poetry, written by emperors, courtiers, ladies-in-waiting, priests, warriors and ordinary people, date from this early period.

During the heyday of the Imperial reign in Kyoto from 794 until 1192, formally judged poetry contests were regular affairs. Ladies and lords of the court regularly communicated in poetry. Poetry writing became an honored profession, with titles and financial rewards bestowed upon the masters of the art.

After the usurpation of national power in 1192 by Yoritomo Minamoto, the first of Japan's shogun warlords, the members of the Imperial family and their huge tree of lineal relatives became a completely leisured class. They subsequently devoted even more time to poetry-writing and other aesthetic pursuits, setting an example for the still larger number of priests as well as the class of professional samurai warriors that developed following the appearance of the shogunate form of government.

The more professional and accomplished the samurai warriors, the more likely they were to take as much pride in their ability to write poetry as in their skill with the arms of their trade. Fatally wounded in battle, ranking warriors would use their last moments of life to compose poems, sometimes expressing their sorrow at leaving life before reaching their goals, other times pillorying their enemies with sharp poetic barbs.

Eventually it became the custom for soldiers about to enter suicidal battles to write "death poems"—a custom followed by the young kamikaze (kah-me-kah-zay) pilots of World War II in the 1940s.

Just as other areas of Japanese life became kata-ized during the nation's long feudal period, the styles and rules of poetry were equally formalized and thereafter contributed significantly to the psychology and behavior of the Japanese. Poetry certainly plays a lesser role in Japanese society today but it remains a popular pastime and each year tens of thousands of people, including members of the Imperial family, participate in a national contest.

BEHIND THE MASKS
OF KABUKI AND NOH

Japanese tendency to kata-ize everything in their lives was epitomized by the kabuki (kah-buu-kee) and noh (no-o) drama forms—the ultimate in method acting. Kabuki is said to have originated in the late 1600s as bawdy dances performed by Shinto shrine "maidens" attached to the Izumo Shrine irv Kyoto. Men eventually replaced all women in kabuki performances after the female dancers became as popular for their sexual services as their entertainment, and attracted the displeasure of the authorities for engaging in unregulated prostitution.

Male actors soon began turning kabuki into a fine art that became more and more formalized and stylized. Over the decades master kabuki stars gradually transformed the craft into the meticulously kata-ized system that is known today.

Once the form and order of movements of kabuki had been established by a master, the style he had created became sanctified. Every movement, down to the blinking of the eyes, was minutely prescribed for all of his disciples.

50

Virtually no personal interpretation were allowed. The challenge for each performer was to follow the kata absolutely. Success was based not only on the artistic interpretation of the plot but also on how precisely the player recreated the set form.

Eventually the style created by the greatest master became the universal kabuki standard and was passed on by him to his chief disciple. This cycle was repeated in each generation. The overall effect was that the kata of kabuki became as important if not more so than the story being told. Noh, Japan's other great drama form, began in the 14th century as part of religious festivals, was to become even more stylized and kata-bound than kabuki. It developed into a form so esoteric that only a limited number of dedicated aficionados are attracted to it.

The essence of noh is for the actor to merge his whole personality into the wooden face mask he wears, to physically and spiritually put himself into the mask, allowing himself to be taken over by the character represented by the mask.

This total sublimation of character and personality into an unchanging wooden mask, and making an art out of it, with the mask becoming both the medium and the message was precisely the goal of all kata—and was characteristic of Japanese culture in general.

Kabuki remains one of the most representative forms of traditional Japanese theater and one of the more impressive examples of the ultimate kata-ization of an art. Performances at Tokyo's famed Kabuki-Za theater, the National Theater and other locations continue to attract large audiences.

Anyone who has difficulty understanding the meaning and point of kata in traditional Japanese culture has only to attend a contemporary presentation of kabuki or noh. More severe foreign critics of the arts say they are virtually devoid of content and are little more than a shell. Even more important, they say, is that Japanese who attend kabuki and noh plays are not aware that most of what they see and hear is form without substance.

"What they are watching is not only meaningless, attending kabuki has become a kata within itself," said one critic.

Of course, this criticism presumes that there is no merit at all in art forms that are kata-ized to this extreme. However, both kabuki and noh are excellent examples of the power of kata in producing illusions, and giving reality to the unreal— both of which are vital ingredients in Japanese culture.

THE BEAUTY CULT

One of the secrets of Japan's commercial prowess is its cultural emphasis on aesthetics. Very early in their history the Japanese developed an acute awareness of the beauty in nature and later developed arts and ceremonies to incorporate the same quality of beauty into their daily lives.

These arts and ceremonies were soon institutionalized into kata with their own aesthetic vocabulary, making it possible for even the least educated person to study and understand aesthetics and make use of the knowledge. It seems that Japan is the only country in the world in which there was a concerted effort on almost every level of society to make the study and appreciation of beauty a basic part of the lifestyle of the entire population.

The roots of the special affinity of the Japanese for aesthetics may have derived from their own native

Shintoism, essentially a worship of nature which incorporated recognition of nature itself as the ultimate source of beauty.

Another part of the Japanese impulse to universalize aestheticism obviously had its origins in Buddhism, as is evidenced in the arts, crafts and lifestyles that developed in other Buddhist countries of Asia. But no other national group took it as far as the Japanese.

It would not be too much of an exaggeration to say that from A.D. 700 on, aestheticsm in Japan took on the appearance and tone of a state religion. Mundane crafts were developed into fine arts. The deliberate pursuit of aesthetic enjoyment became a major theme in the lives of the more affluent. The practice of one or more aesthetic skills became the norm and was expected of virtually all Japanese, regardless of their economic status.

Japanese aesthetic pursuits were designed to pleasure all of the senses as well as the spirit. They included such formalized practices as poetry-writing, moon-viewing, cherry blossom-viewing, incense parties, sightseeing, listening to the songs of insects, flower arranging, music, folk dancing, and the tea ceremony.

By the beginning of Japan's modern industrial era in the 1870s the Japanese had been immersed in an aesthetically oriented culture for well over one thousand years. The exercise of a highly refined aesthetic sense was second nature to them and was reflected in all their endeavors, from the weaving of baskets to the production of wrapping paper and soup bowls.

Unfortunately it was to be nearly one hundred years before the Japanese of the modern era could take full advantage of their aesthetic skills insofar as their export industries were concerned. Most of the foreign traders who began flocking to Japan soon after the country was opened to the West in the 1850s were more interested in cheap labor and the ability of the Japanese to copy foreign products than they were in their aesthetic sense or skills in producing beautiful handicrafts.

Following the end of World War II in 1945, the number of foreign buyers pouring into Japan to order cheaply made Western style products became a flood. For the next decade the quality of what the Japanese produced for export was almost totally controlled by foreign buyers whose primary aim was to make as much profit as possible as quickly as possible.

As soon as Japanese makers could wrest control of their production from foreign importers, first by opening their own import offices abroad and then by establishing their own sales networks, they began to upgrade the quality of their products in keeping with their own traditions. Within ten years, the Japanese were renowned world-wide for the superior quality of their exports.

It was to be another ten years before Western businessmen began to show an interest in *why* and *how* the Japanese were producing such high quality merchandise.

I believe Japan's aesthetic concepts of *shibui* (she-buu-ee), *wabi* (wah-bee) and *sabi* (sah-bee) should be incorporated into all cultures. Sabi refers to a kind of beauty that comes with the natural aging of all things; wabi to an emotional appreciation that reflects the essence, including the ephemeral quality, of life; and shibui denotes beauty that results when an object, natural or man-made, clearly reveals its essence through perfection of form, naturalness, simplicity and subdued tone.

THE ART OF BOWING

The bow is one of the most conspicuous symbols of Japan's vertically oriented superior-inferior society, of Japanese etiquette, and the importance of social kata in general. Its traditional importance went well beyond simple conformity and good manners. It was a significant part of both the physical and psychological conditioning of the Japanese in their whole culture.

Until the 1950s virtually all Japanese got their first training in bowing while they were still infants, strapped to their mothers' backs. Every time their mothers bowed, the babies bowed with them.

Bowing correctly for different occasions is far more complicated and meaningful than the casual visitor might suspect. As in everything Japanese there is a kata for bowing, with only one right way for each occasion. One must know when to bow as well as what kind of bow is correct for a variety of situations. The wrong kind of bow can be a very serious infraction with dire consequences. In earlier times it could be fatal.

The right kind of bow is determined by such things as the relative ages of the participants, their personal and/or professional relationship, their past experience, their purpose in meeting, and so on.

Older Japanese, particularly those who are worried about the erosion of the Japanese Way, are especially concerned that Japan's younger generations are not being taught how or why to bow by their parents. As a result, many Japanese companies, especially those in the retail and service industries, now include bowing in their training programs. Some in the past have gone so far as to use a special bowing device to help new employees get the proper angle down pat.

Part of the worry of Japanese traditionalists is recognition that those who are not fully indoctrinated in bowing at a very young age have already lost a vital aspect of their Japaneseness and will not regain it with a few days or weeks of training in the kata of bowing. These conservatives understand that the bow is part of the behavioral conditioning that makes the Japanese Japanese and helps hold the traditional culture together.

Despite the tendency of young Japanese parents to spend less time training their children in the age-old custom of bowing it remains a vital factor in the adult world of Japan and most of Japan's major companies are determined to keep it that way. Many companies have kata-ized training programs specially designed to wipe out the modernized personalities of new young employees and remake them in the traditional mold.

The remolding and character-building training programs of many large Japanese companies are very intense. Some of them are degrading to the point that the previously pampered young recruits are shocked. These training schools require new employees to do such things as wash out toilets bowls and clean up after sick drunks.

The primary purpose of these company and special schools is not to teach practical subjects, but to condition the recruits in the traditional social etiquette still rigidly followed in the business world, and to instill in them deep feelings of loyalty and devotion to the company. Such training, which is usually very expensive, also makes it perfectly clear to the new employees that the company is equally devoted to them.

This generally arduous, mutually shared training creates a special bond among the recruits and between them and the company managers who often participate in the programs as instructors. The close ties they form become a significant factor in the personal relationships of each new crop of recruits over their thirty-five to forty-year working lives. In addition to acting as mentors to their younger colleagues, Japanese managers also routinely arranged marriages for them and served as key speakers at their weddings.

[One of the foreign-Japanese equivalents of mutually endured trials of strength, stamina, dedication and determination are the long hours of drinking and carousing in bars and cabarets after working hours that is required to forge close bonds with Japanese businessmen.

Building and sustaining close relationships in this manner represent one of the most expensive aspects of business in Japan—not only in terms of the financial cost but in emotional and time investment as well. Another mutual ordeal is playing golf when you have to travel several hours each way to get to a course and it is raining or freezing cold during the entire outing.]

Many Japanese company managers look upon college graduates with liberal arts degrees as ignorant, unreliable and virtually worthless until they are whipped into shape at the company boot camp. In some companies this "dirty work" training lasts for several months, and only those who survive the course are accepted into the companies as regular staff members.

Except for new recruits schooled in technical skills, managers do not look for the most intelligent, most ambitious or the most energetic employee candidates. In fact young people who fit these categories may not fit into the typical company system in Japan. Many managers look first for young people who do not have strongly held opinions or ambitions and can be molded into what the managers regard as company soldiers—people who will adhere strictly to the military-like hierarchy of the Japanese company, obey rules without question, and devote their lives to working diligently and rising slowly in the ranks.

Major Japanese companies generally depend upon professors with whom they have strong ties to select the graduating seniors with engineering and other technical degrees that they hire each year. In most instances these professors literally decide on their own which student is going to what company

Until the 1980s female employees were usually excluded from the male bastion of management in Japanese companies, and were generally not required to undergo "boot-camp" training. Their training usually ended with how to sit, how to stand before superiors, how to respond with the proper speech, how to bow and how to serve tea. Not surprisingly, Japanese women bow more often than Japanese men.

THE ART OF AMBIGUITY

Another kata-ized formula that the Japanese have traditionally polished to perfection is the "art of ambiguity," which was developed to avoid commitments, disagreements and responsibility, and to help maintain a facade of harmony. It is also used to keep outsiders, competitors and enemies uncertain and, therefore, at a considerable disadvantage.

Japan's cultural imperative to maintain harmony and promote group consensus by the use of ambiguous language had a fundamental effect on the nature and use of the Japanese language itself. The demands of non-confrontational wa not only influenced the way the language was used, it also contributed to the appearance of new words and word endings.

The Japanese can and do, in fact, communicate clearly, candidly and even bluntly to members of their own families, close friends and subordinates. But they are inclined go into an ambiguous mode when confronted by anyone else. Reason for this, according to Jiro Kamishima, professor emeritus of St. Paul's University in Tokyo and a noted cultural historian, is that the Japanese suffer from a phobia about being isolated in any manner, physical or otherwise (Japan Foundation Newsletter, Vol. 17, No. 3).

Professor Kamishima says that the Japanese use ambiguity as a security device to prevent themselves from being caught in a minority position. He says they dread isolation from the mainstream so much that they refrain from expressing themselves clearly or taking a stand until a majority position gradually emerges. They are evasive, Professor Kamishima adds, because they lack confidence in themselves, and feel that the *seken no me* (say-kane no may) or "eyes of the world" are on them at all times. "They are obsessed with the idea that they must converge (their thinking)," he says.

This is no doubt one of the factors that was responsible for the development of the famous *tatemae* (tah-tay-my) and *honne* (hoan-nay) concepts in Japanese behavior. Tatemae refers to a front or facade (public statements) that people put up to obscure their real meaning and intentions (honne). It is also the reason why the Japanese are obsessed with seeking more and more information and endlessly asking for advice from experts and authority figures.

Because of this character, typical Japanese tend to be followers rather than leaders, going whichever way the leaning of their group directs them—and herein lies one of the dangers inherent in Japan's kata-ized culture. Like sheep, the Japanese are subject to being misled, either by misinformation or by a wolf in sheep's clothing. They are also prone to stampede in one direction or another as the result of a single incident. Their proclivity for jumping into fads is a part of this character.

The most frightening manifestation of this herd-like behavior is in the actions of Japan's mass media, which routinely tailor their approach to the news to conform to preconceived notions of what is "Japanese" or what is best for Japan. Generally speaking, individual news media that find themselves out of step with the majority will quickly fall in line if they come under sustained criticism.

Ability in using language ambiguously while still getting your point across remains one of the most important social, business and political skills in Japan. Much of the famed *hara gei* (hah-rah gay-e) or "art of the stomach" that the Japanese use in their personal as well as business relationships fits within the kata of ambiguity. Hara gei is a highly honed emotional and intuitive ability that often cannot be expressed in words. It functions more or less like cultural telepathy, and is usually incomprehensible to those who are not similarly skilled.

"Cultural homogeneity makes it possible for the Japanese to communicate with each other without expressing their thoughts clearly or completely," noted American businessman-writer Davis Barrager. "Their comments and conversations are also regularly punctuated by blank spaces that leave the uninitiated listener hanging but convey volumes of unspoken thoughts to those who are on the Japanese wavelength," he added.

This style of communication has been recognized and

categorized for centuries. It involves the use of *ma* (man), pregnant pauses, or "leaving space" that the listener is expected to fill in with his or her own interpretation of what the speaker means. Misunderstandings are a natural outcome when someone is unskilled at this kind of cultural decoding.

Barrager continued: "Many common Japanese words convey superficial meanings that mask reality. You must let communication with the Japanese run its course until something concrete emerges and then deal with it. Americans like myself, with our frontier traditions of dealing summarily with new situations, instinctively want to shift quickly through the chaff and go straight to the wheat. Usually that does not work in Japan, even when the Japanese want something as soon as possible. Generally you must let the chaff shift at its own pace."

When the Japanese are operating in their own cultural world, among themselves, they are often not aware of their use of ambiguity and time gaps. Most such behavior is automatic. Ambiguity is so natural and accepted that they generally don't conceptualize it, and often cannot comprehend why foreigners have such difficulty understanding them.

In formal situations, however, the Japanese are generally very much aware of the role of gaps in speech and ambiguity in all of their nuances, and are variously skilled in their use. The deliberate use of this manner of communication has traditionally played a key role in virtually all of Japan's international relations, and remains an important factor today.

Of course, most Westerners who have contact with the Japanese are not skilled in the use of ambiguity or gaps in communication, do not accept it as normal and are confused and upset by it. This means that physically as well as emotionally, Japanese and non-Japanese are indeed often on different wavelengths.

There are other factors at play that make ambiguous behavior by the Japanese appear as irrational and often devious to the outsider when they have no intention of being or appearing illogical or deceitful. This again is part of the process of group-think and decision by consensus. During the investigation period of any project or program, no one in the group knows exactly where everyone is in the process. They cannot be precise in their comments or predict the outcome.

When judged by Western standards, the uncertainty and indecisiveness of the Japanese when they are in the midst of establishing a consensus adds substantially to their reputation for ambiguity and makes their behavior seem even more suspect.

Further, while Japanese find the use of ambiguity helpful in maintaining surface harmony and in keeping foreigners outside of their inner circle, the price they pay is high. It is emotionally demanding, and at least for those who have become partly de-Japanized it is often frustrating as well.

IMPORTANCE OF THE APOLOGY

Japan's feudal society was so hedged in by rigorously enforced rules of etiquette that it was virtually impossible for a person to get through any day without breaking at least one rule or rubbing someone the wrong way. The ritualized and sanctified manners also made the Japanese extremely sensitive to any deviation from this code of conduct, and ready to take offense at the vaguest hint of a slight or insult.

Just opening a conversation with someone other than a member of the household or a friend became a sensitive matter because it implied the possibility of creating some kind of obligation or invading the other person's privacy.

In a *ying-yang* kind of move to balance the demands of the etiquette system—as well as the often inhumanly harsh punishments meted out to the more serious offenders—the kata of the apology were institutionalized and made a significant part of daily life.

It became customary for people to apologize in advance—before a comment or action—just in case they might inadvertently upset someone or make a mistake. So common was the practice of the apology that one of the words used for "thank you" was also used to mean "excuse me" or "I'm sorry." This word—*sumimasen* (sue-me-mah-sin)—literally means "it never ends." In other words, "my imposition on you never ends."

More serious apologies were naturally formalized with their own *kata,* with different styles of apologies for different classes and groups of people. Yakuza (yah-kuu-zah), or the professional gangsters of Japan, have traditionally apol- ogized for serious transgressions against their bosses or other powerful figures *by* cutting off part of a finger—usually the first joint of the little finger on the left hand. If a second apology is required, the tip of the little finger on the right hand is cut off.

Until the turn of the century it was still common in Japan to see yakuza with pieces of little fingers missing, mingling with other guests in certain international hotels and night spots.

Following the industrialization of Japan in the 1870s and

80s, the apology became so important in the conduct of business that many companies employed professionals who specialized in apologizing in person as well as writing letters of apology.

Still today company managers who are especially skilled at apologizing are regularly assigned this task when the need arises. Besides having polished verbal skills, these expert apologizers must also be very good at performing the proper kind of bows and in selecting and presenting consolation gifts or money. The kata of the apology are therefore another critical factor in the complex conditioning that goes into the molding of a Japanese.

Despite their overuse, apologies carry considerable moral weight in Japan. The guilty individual who apologizes sincerely is often forgiven for relatively serious transgressions. By the same token, refusing to apologize or withholding an apology can be very serious. In legal matters, refusing to express regret invariably results in heavier punishment. In personal situations, it typically results in acts of revenge.

One of my foreign friends recounted a common experience, this one involving his mother. Out driving one day she made a wrong turn and was stopped by the police. When it turned out that she had inadvertently let her license expire, the case became serious. Her husband, his employer and the American Embassy became involved. Things looked grim until a police officer came up with a compromise that let everyone save face. He told my friend's mother that all would be forgiven if she would write out an apology and promise never to drive in Japan again.

The police officer then wisely added that it might come to pass that she would want to start driving again, but that no one could predict the future. He was giving her the opportunity to renew her license and carry on.

BIG BROTHER AND GROUPISM

Japan's social ethic during the feudal age was based on principles derived from Confucianism. All household and group members were collectively responsible for each other's actions. All could be, and frequently were, punished for the transgressions of one member.

This draconian system, designed to force absolute obedience to laws and kata-ized customs, contributed immeasurably to family consciousness and loyalty to the group, to passivity, and to robotic behavior. The crowding factor also made unified actions necessary, resulting in the Japanese tendency to move as groups in unison.

Each kata-ized group protected itself by threatening to ostracize any member who failed to follow prescribed behavior—a fate that was generally regarded as worse than death because other groups would normally not take an outsider in. The group thus defined and controlled the individual. In many ways any individual not a member of a recognized group simply did not exist.

Groupism is still a very significant facet of Japanese life. It prevails in every profession, in business and in politics. In most cases, getting acquainted and dealing with the Japanese professionally means getting acquainted and dealing with them not only as individuals but also as groups, with the group taking precedence over the individual.

In business dealings in particular it is vital to meet and nurture relationships with several individuals in the same company. Trying to work through just one person almost always fails.

The group, now as in the past, provides security and economic survival. There is relentless pressure for people to join groups and stay in them. One of the ways a group binds its members together is the sharing of personal, intimate information. Anyone who disregards this rule is suspect and the more conspicuous violators are likely to be ostracized.

THE WAY OF SUICIDE

To Westerners probably the most bizarre and shocking facet of feudal Japan's kata culture was the practice of ritual suicide, called seppuku (sep-puu-kuu)—or harakiri (hah-rah-kee-ree) in colloquial terms.

Harakiri was developed by the samurai class as a way for members to dispatch themselves when they faced capture by an enemy, when they ran afoul of their own lord or the shogunate and were ordered to kill themselves, or when they became involved in some kind of personal conflict for which there was no other acceptable alternative.

The terms seppuku and harakiri literally mean "cutting the stomach." This mode of suicide was chosen by the samurai because it required extraordinary will, courage and strength to accomplish. A short sword was inserted into the stomach on the left side. Using both hands the sword was drawn to the right side of the stomach, then pulled upward, forming an angle or L-shaped cut.

Such a deep cut through the stomach was intensely painful, but it was usually several minutes to hours before the victims died. As time passed, it became common to provide for a quicker and less painful death by having an assistant stand to the side of the victim and severe his head with a sword immediately after the stomach cut was made.

In keeping with their highly kata-ized lifestyle, the samurai made harakiri into an equally formalized "art" that was as carefully and minutely programmed as a stage production. Every aspect of the suicide was detailed, from the white paper used to wrap around the part of the sword blade held by the hands to the last poems the victims wrote before self-immolation. Administrative castles such as the soaring "white heron" hill castle of Himeji had special inner "courts" for the ritual of suicide—appropriately labeled *HamkiriMaru* (Hah-rah-kee-ree Mah-ruu) or "Stomach-cutting courts."

All official suicides required witnesses. The higher ranked the individual, the more people invited to attend the ritual. In 1868 Lord Redesdale, a British diplomat, and six other foreigners were invited to attend the suicide of a 32-year-old samurai from the province of Bizen who had ordered Japanese soldiers to fire on the foreign settlement in Hyogo (Kobe).

Lord Redesdale later recounted the experience in his book, *Tales of Old Japan,* the first description by a foreigner of this remarkable way of life and death. The foreign witnesses were both shocked and fascinated by the scene.

Harakiri was so entrenched during the long Tokugawa era (1603-1868) that repeated edicts by the various clan lords and shoguns prohibiting the practice were ignored. While uncommon today, the tradition of ritual suicide remains a discernible element in Japanese society, in attitude if not in practice.

The custom of harakiri, perhaps more than anything

else, starkly reveals the depth and intensity of Japan's traditional codified culture and helps explain the reason why it was able to mold the Japanese into such a distinctive society.

THE KATA-IZED MIND

The introduction of industrialism into Japan from the 1860s and the disappearance of the samurai class after 1868 did not mean the end of the kata culture that had been so carefully and thoroughly nurtured for so many centuries. It was too much a part of the spirit of the Japanese to be so easily discarded.

The philosophy of the shikata system was an integral part of Japanese thinking, expressed not only in the use of their language but also in many of their deeply rooted habits and customs. It was the core of what made the Japanese *Japanese*. Virtually all of their attitudes and reactions, which foreigners tended to find either delightful or deplorable, emanated from this all-encompassing kata conditioning.

Japanese could not help but think in terms of shikata. It was this conditioning that was to make them formidable enemies in war and even more formidable competitors in commerce in the decades ahead.

3

KATA IN JAPAN TODAY

CONTINUING THE KATA CULTURE

At the end of Japan's feudal period in 1868, the custom of kata-izing all skills and behavior permeated virtually every aspect of Japanese life. The way to prepare and serve food was structured and codified. The way to hold chopsticks was rigidly prescribed. There was a set place to lay chopsticks when they were not in use. There was only one proper way to hold a tea cup or sake cup and a prescribed way to drink.

Clothing was worn in a certain way that was taught as carefully as one teaches an art. There was a right way to fold and store clothing. There was a right way to dust, to scrub floors. There was a right way to hold and use a fan. There was a right way to walk. There was virtually no area of Japanese life that did not have a specific form and order.

Any action or behavior that did not follow the prescribed form was not only uneducated and uncultured, it was *un*-Japanese and therefore anti-Japanese—and by extension anti-Japan.

The downfall of Japan's last great feudal dynasty did not end the role of kata in education and training. In fact, the training system, which previously had centered on the samurai class and embodied many major kata, was quickly broadened to include the mass of common people as well.

During this period, universal education was made

the law of the land. In addition to mastering all of the life-style skills in language and behavior that had been kata-ized for centuries, the lower classes also were now required to undergo the rigorous training necessary to master thousands of Kan-Ji.

The country's newly organized Western-style military forces, made up of commoner soldiers and sailors, usually commanded by former samurai, were formidable examples of kata in action. The armed forces were taught how to fight and how to die—but not how to surrender. [Some seventy-five years later the end of World War II was probably delayed by several weeks because there was no kata for doing something that was virtually unthinkable. Some officers, quoted by Japanese author Hatsuho Naito in *The Thundergods* (the story of Japan's World War II kamikaze corps), who wanted to end the carnage bemoaned this lack, exclaiming, "We don't know *how* to surrender!"]

Many of the other kata that were traditional in Japan for centuries were also carried over into modern times—some on a substantially lesser scale, but nevertheless to the extent that they make a measureable contribution to the skill levels and cultural coherence of the country today.

All of the massive efforts to transform the country from a cottage industry economy into an industrialized nation by importing Western ideas and systems during the 1870s and 1880s were filtered through the fabric of Japan's cultural kata, with the result that the country was modernized, but not Westernized.

Some of the kata-based skills from the past which remain in place today include the tea ceremony, flower arranging, kendo, judo and other sports. There is a

Japanized way to arrange furniture and office desks, for learning how to drive, for treating guests, for buying and presenting gifts, and so on.

Even the several billion dollars spent each year in the country's hostess clubs and bars by businessmen on expense accounts is a form of kata, says a female Japanese executive. "Most of the money is spent to impress customers and contacts, to obligate them and to build personal relationships that can be turned into business. It is not for fun or because they enjoy the company of the individuals involved. It is deliberate and carefully designed, with its own form and process", she said.

Japan's professional criminal class, the yakuza, have specific kata of their own that make them instantly recognizable to most Japanese. Yakuza kata covers their speech, the way they walk, their dress—even their hair style, with distinct variations based on where they live in Japan. Typical yakuza wear pin-striped suits, black shirts with gaudy designs on them, lots of expensive jewelry including gold chains, pendants and lapel pins; have flat-top crew cuts or short Afro-style curls; walk with a swagger, talk roughly, are argumentative and generally behave in an arrogant manner. Some sixty to seventy percent of yakuza have colorful tattoos that cover most of their bodies.

THE ROLE OF MARTIAL ARTS

Martial arts have had an extraordinary influence on the creation and maintenance of Japan's kata culture because of the development and long ascendancy of the professional samurai warrior class. Several of these arts, particularly judo and kendo, remain today an important part of the mental and physical conditioning of a significant segment of the male population.

Japan's modern sport of judo was derived from the ancient martial art known as *jujutsu* (juu-jute-sue). Following the downfall of the Tokugawa shogunate government in 1868 and the subsequent dissolution of the samurai warrior class, many of the schools teaching fighting arts to the samurai were closed. Within a short time, however, martial arts schools open to the general public began to appear.

A Tokyo University student named Jigoro Kano got the idea of developing a form of jujutsu that anyone could practice as a character builder. In 1882 he opened the now famous Kodo Kan School of Judo and began promoting the new sport.

Kano changed the purpose of the art from disabling or killing an opponent to developing mental and physical control of the body and imbuing students with strong bodies, strong wills, high moral values and adherence to traditional samurai-style etiquette.

Kano's new version of an old deadly fighting art grew steadily. Eventually it was introduced into regular schools as part of the curriculum, and also became part of the training at Japan's police academies. Now, as judo, it is a major worldwide sport.

While only a small percentage of all Japanese take up judo in school or as part of their profession—as in the case of police and the military—its influence is felt on a much broader basis because those who seriously practice the skill often develop the kind of character that contributes to their success in later life. The profiles of Japanese businessmen, in particular, show a higher than average percentage who practiced judo in their youth.

It is interesting to note that several hundred thousand Westerners have undergone intensive conditioning in Japanese kata since the 1960s, some of them without realizing the cultural significance, and the number continues to grow each year. These partially kata-ized Westerners are students of Japan's famed karate-do (kah-rah-tay-doe)—and most of them are good examples of the positive aspects of the kata system.

Karate-do, or "way of the empty hand/' refers to a method of fighting based on using the hands and feet instead of weaponry. The earliest forms of "empty hand" fighting were created in China by Buddhist priests for self-protection during the Tang Dynasty (A.D. 618-907).

Priests (and other common people) in China were prevented by Imperial law from owning and using any kind of weapon. Yet they were subjected to frequent attacks by brigands, the soldiers of warring lords, and various kinds of ruffians. Strong-minded priests developed the art of karate (as well as what is known in the West as *kung fn)* to protect themselves. Over the centuries the techniques of karate were expanded and polished into a highly sophisticated and deadly martial art.

In the 14th century, traveling Buddhist priests intro-duced karate to the island kingdom of Okinawa, now a prefecture of Japan, located about seven hundred kilometers south of the main islands of Japan. Karate thrived among the Okinawans but it was not until 1922 that it was finally introduced into mainland Japan.

As they generally do with all imports, the Japanese modified and Japanized karate, incorporating techniques and training methods from aiki-do (aye-kee doe) and jujutsu both of which dated back to the 11th century and the rise of the samurai military class.

Also as is typical in Japan, several schools of karate were soon formed by masters who favored slightly different techniques. The art spread rapidly among the discipline-minded Japanese, and from the 1950s began to attract the attention of many Westerners. Karate-do gyms can now be found all over the world, and the sport represents one of Japan's most successful exports.

In its modernized form, karate is divided into three distinct categories: (1) a set of defensive and offensive *kumite* (kuu-me-tay) or moves that are carefully detailed; (2) "free" moves, for offense as well as defense, in which practitioners may innovate; and (3) kata or "form" practice. Both of the kumite categories require an opponent, while kata are practiced alone.

The third category, kata, is the foundation of all karate training. Besides teaching the established basic moves, these kata are designed to condition the mind and the body of the student in an overall way of life. They incorporate control of the emotions, self-confidence, a strong spirit, respect for others, a sophisticated etiquette, plus a highly disciplined control of the body as it is put through a series of finitely structured moves performed at high speed.

Karate students cannot advance in rank without achieving considerable skill in the philosophy and discipline of the art. Schools normally will not teach the deadlier facets of karate to anyone who does not understand and accept the philosophy and discipline that goes with it.

Karate is thus a perfect example of Japanese kata in action in an ideal situation based on total control of the mind and body, absolute adherence to minutely prescribed behavior, the mastery of techniques designed to mount a perfect defense or demolish an opponent, and a moral philosophy that integrates peace and power.

SURVIVAL LINKED WITH KATA

Continuation of Japan's kata culture was guaranteed when the traits resulting from the kata were directly linked to the industrialized economy which the new Meiji government sponsored from 1868 on. First, the level of schooling was made the primary qualification for employment, with the best jobs reserved exclusively for those who were better educated. Second, individuals who did not conform to the traditional way in both attitudes and behavior were rejected by the higher levels of the system. Organizations of all types simply weeded out candidates who did not fit the national mold.

Japan's tightly knit group orientation did not encourage individual entrepreneurship that might lead to conspicuous success by either the uneducated or social mavericks outside of the system. The relationship between kata-ized education and success in life became the overriding factor in the new Japanese society. Official freedom to upgrade their social class through academic and economic success, virtually for the first time in the history of the country, gave the Japanese an extraordinary will to succeed despite the personal constraints.

Elementary and high school level education in Japan was naturally structured with very specific kata that ranged from identical uniforms and bowing to strict routines for classroom performance. The system was designed to mold each student into a homogenized product of the culture. The only screen for public college admissions was a standardized test. No consideration was given to school grades, extracurricular activities or anything else.

The overall result of all Japanese being subjected to a strict molding process during childhood and their teen years developed a common set of "Japanese" characteristics that were thereafter to play a seminal role in the country's future, more so than in the past because this time the system was applied to everyone, not just the privileged classes. These characteristics included:

1) A highly developed sense of balance, form, order and style.
2) An intuitive feel (and need) for precision, accuracy and correctness.
3) Extraordinary manual dexterity and the ability to work especially well on small, sophisticated things.
4) A predisposition to apply themselves with single-minded dedication to the task at hand.
5) An overwhelming desire to excel in anything they did; to be as good as or better than anyone else—although if they were better than members of their own group they had to downplay their talent behind a mask of humility in order to maintain internal harmony.

Exhibiting pride in one's ability or accomplishments has always been taboo in Japan, and it is common to see noted people humble themselves before their colleagues and the public. There were no restraints on competing with other Japanese groups or foreigners, however, with the result that groups within companies as well as companies compete fiercely against each other. "No holds are barred. It is dog-eat-dog as long as a facade of harmony is maintained," said a resident foreign businessman.

In fact, within the context of their group the Japanese

are virtually obsessed with being better and doing things better than outsiders, and are constantly making comparisons. Books written by foreigners trumpeting Japan's successes in comparison with other countries are especially popular among the Japanese. The news media constantly reinforces the theme that the Japanese are a superior people.

In addition to the Japanese compulsion to excel as groups it also became characteristic for each individual within a group to give his all for the group. The tendency was for each person to accept total responsibility for the goals of the group and do his utmost to achieve them. This results in an extraordinary amount of energy and synergy being applied to any project.

As can readily be appreciated, an entire nation physically and mentally conditioned in these attributes is going to have a significant advantage over people who are less trained, especially when their efforts are channeled by the government and industry to achieve specific goals.

Despite the closed-in nature of the conditioning undergone by Japanese—or perhaps because of it—they have an eclectic mentality. As a rule they are fascinated by foreign things and ideas, and have an innate compulsion to analyze and digest everything that comes their way. This compulsion covers everything from clothing and food to technology, and contributed greatly to the economic and social strides they have made since 1868. Among other things, Japanese will sample any food, any fad, and if they like it they add it to their repertoire without any strain on their cultural character.

This explains why there are so many French-style pastry shops in Japan...some in busy train stations.

YOUNGER GENERATIONS LOSING STEAM!

THE COMPULSION FOR QUALITY

Over the centuries all Japanese were programmed with the idea that every service they performed or product they made had to precisely follow kata whose goals were perfection. No allowances were made for anything less. Time and cost were not primary considerations. Some of the more famous artists and designers of the day would not accept any project that had money or time constraints. This attitude remains characteristic of the Japanese today.

While virtually all Japanese workers are thus bound by the bun and kata of their occupation—as well as their identity as Japanese—to do whatever is necessary to make the best product possible, many Western workers have been conditioned to do the minimum possible to get by.

As mentioned earlier, the quality of virtually everything the Japanese made for export from 1870 until 1960 was strictly controlled by foreign importers who brought in the samples to be copied, designated the materials to be used and set the prices. Japanese looked upon these products with contempt regarding them as suitable only for foreigners with no taste or quality standards.

Present-day Japanese are, of course, noted for their concern—some might say obsession—with quality, which is still another example of an important factor inherited from their kata-based culture. Their long history of kata-ized arts, crafts and general lifestyle conditioned them to automatically expect the highest possible level of quality in any service or product.

In keeping with the best of their cultural conditioning, the Japanese began institutionalizing the concept of quality in modern or Western style products during the 1950s, and within a decade the whole process had been as kata-ized and sanctified as the crafting of traditional ceramics, lacquer-ware and pottery.

One of the aspects of the quality obsession of the Japanese is that it covers the whole product, including areas that are not ordinarily seen—the bottom, inside, and so on. Many Western products have failed the Japanese test for quality because they were not fully finished or detailed.

JAPANESE-STYLE SINCERITY

Early visitors to Japan were singularly struck by the degree of sincerity, faithfulness and fidelity of the typical Japanese—to family, friends and employers. The average employee would not cheat his employer or stint on his efforts despite lack of supervision or control. For the most part, dedication to duty and responsibility transcended personal considerations.

Present-day Japanese commentators point out that in many other societies it is taken for granted that human nature is evil and if not controlled will automatically resort to evil deeds—a belief that is usually self-fulfilling. In contrast, they say, traditionally oriented Japanese are intrinsically good and if left unsupervised will continue to work diligently, voluntarily trying to improve the quality of their work as well as their productivity.

Changing mores in Japan have frayed this traditional Japanese trait of self-motivated performance, but enough of it remains to be very conspicuous and to be one of the primary advantages the Japanese have over most other societies.

The sincerity and diligence of the Japanese is not a casual or amorphous thing. It is a structured, learned behavior that they take notice of and pride in. They habitually make comparisons between Japanese and foreigners, noting that

Japanese are more diligent and more sincere than foreigners—while tending to ignore any evidence to the contrary.

A typical example of this behavior: At 6 a.m. in a New York hotel coffee shop where I had just finished an early breakfast I met the sales manager of a major Japanese company whom I knew from Tokyo. I made the casual comment, "You're up early this morning!"—a common greeting. The man very seriously replied, "Because I am a diligent Japanese!"

His tone of voice and manner implied very emphatically that other people did not get up early because they were not diligent and did not measure up to Japanese standards. He simply did not recognize that I and many other non-Japanese were also up and busy.

It seems that sincerity has several distinct meanings to Japanese. A basic meaning is to never deceive one's self or others; to have harmony within one's inner self and with all interaction with others; to precisely follow proper etiquette with the appropriate demeanor. Another meaning is to be constantly ready to give up everything in order to behave in a totally spontaneous way in response to one's innermost feelings. Such spontaneous behavior, when it occurs, can be either glorious or shocking, depending on its content.

As in all things Japanese, there is a specific, recognizable kata to Japanese sincerity. The fundamental ethic of Japanese style sincerity is that people adhere faithfully to all expected behavior; that no action be taken that would result in others losing face; that decisions and actions reflect the will and needs of the group; that harmony prevail. Other key ingredients in Japanese sincerity include honesty, "wholehearted-ness," "warmth," and the special Japanese characteristic called *ganbari no seishin* (gahn-bah-ree no say-e-sheen) or "never give-up spirit."

Demonstrating Japanese-style sincerity requires that one follow the kata of Japanese etiquette and spirit in all things—eating, sitting, meeting people, talking, working and responding properly to all the passages of life, from births and weddings to deaths.

The power of the kata of sincerity is demonstrated daily in all areas of life in Japan, sometimes with tragic consequences. One example dating from the 1980s: five girls in a junior high school in Fukuoka were arrested and charged with bullying a classmate into committing suicide. When the five 14-year-olcl girls were asked why they bullied their classmate into killing herself they said it was because she had "failed to be sincere enough" when attending a funeral ceremony for the mother of one of the five girls.

Studies have shown that Japanese business managers believe sincerity takes precedence over all other values in management, while American and European managers consider fairness the most important value. The next most important management value in the Japanese context of things is "the spirit of challenge," meaning that the individual is dedicated to giving his all to overcoming any obstacle and surpassing all others in achievement.

Because Japanese sincerity is based on a situational etiquette instead of universal principles, however, there is another side to it—an opposite, with parallel kata for being insincere when it suits their purpose. These kata include not saying what they really think, pretending that things are fine when they really are not, and ignoring things and people for self-serving reasons. This factor alone brings a very subtle nuance to interpersonal relationships in Japan, and makes it especially difficult for foreigners to have confidence in their dealings with Japanese.

BUILDING TRUST

The *shinyo* (sheen-yoe) or "trust" factor in Japanese society is an extension of the sincerity factor. Without sincerity one cannot have shinyo, and without trust one cannot build or maintain a long-lasting personal or business relationship. Trust, the Japanese say, is the end result of sincere behavior.

Japanese are extraordinarily sensitive about "losing face," but this sensitivity often takes a backseat to their concern for trust. As is frequently noted, you can lose face any number of times and survive, and face is relatively easy to regain— sometimes in a matter of minutes or hours with some new success or redeeming behavior. But loss of trust is extremely difficult to overcome and there are many occasions when it is simply impossible to regain. As the Japanese say, not being trusted is like having a thousand and one enemies.

There is no mystery about how to build shinyo. In broad terms one does everything possible to avoid disrupting harmony, causing someone else to lose face or giving anyone reason for doubting your sincerity. In specific terms one builds trust by keeping all promises and commitments. In business terms this means keeping delivery dates, responding to complaints promptly and positively, making prompt repairs and carrying out after-sales services.

It also includes minimizing price hikes, notifying your business partners in advance of any planned changes and seeking their understanding and cooperation, continuously striving to improve the quality of your products or services, and helping your business partners—clients or customers—if they get into trouble because of circumstances beyond their control.

People who consistently behave in this manner command the trust and respect of all and can often get cooperation and help from Japanese companies that go beyond ordinary business considerations. The kata of shinyo is nothing more than always following the highest Japanese-style moral and etiquette standards prescribed by the Japanese Way.

Not surprisingly, it is very difficult for foreigners to establish the kind and level of trust with the Japanese that they expect among themselves. Some life-long foreign residents of Japan say it is impossible. They point out that the foreigner simply cannot guarantee that harmony will not be disrupted, and that the record of foreigners dealing with Japan proves the point as far as the Japanese are concerned.

By the same token, it is common for Japanese companies to take advantage of individual foreign businessmen as well as foreign companies, no matter how sincere the foreigners are in their attempts to follow the kata of trust and loyalty demanded by the Japanese. Often, their rationale is that it is alright to take such advantage because the foreigners are not Japanese and such behavior is therefore acceptable.

This kind of logic is not applied only to foreigners, however. It is also applied to other Japanese, usually covertly but other times openly as well, especially when no group ties are involved. "The Japanese play hardball against all outsiders. Their policy is, If you have the hammer you hit the other guy at the first opportunity/" said a foreign business-man with long experience in Japan.

WINNING BY THE NUMBERS

Japanese are culturally conditioned to win and typically

continue trying to win even though they know they are going to lose. They feel compelled to persevere because of the obligation they owe to their position and role in society, says Japanese writer Takashi Iwasaki. This obligation is especially strong when the individual concerned is high-ranking—in the military, in business or in government—but it pertains to a degree to all Japanese regardless of their status. Ultimately, their identity as Japanese compels them to sacrifice themselves to fulfill the role they perceive as required to uphold the honor of the country.

This obligation to win or succeed in whatever endeavor concerned is, as always, group-oriented, but it is common for individuals of rank to assume responsibility personally when the matter is grave and on a large scale.

Westerners dealing with the Japanese invariably encounter this "must-win" tactic. In virtually all relationships it is predicated on the concept of continuing to talk and question (negotiate) in a very polite but tenacious manner until the other side compromises and a consensus is reached or the other side is worn down and gives up. This technique is particularly conspicuous in business as well as in political and diplomatic negotiations.

One veteran foreign negotiator observed that, generally speaking, the Japanese are exceptionally reserved and polite when they are in a weak position, but he added: "In my experience they are less polite and can be rapacious when they have the advantage."

Japanese typically employ a number of other deeply entrenched cultural characteristics in using their hang-in kata, particularly patience and pliancy—bending with the wind without losing their essence or form—and a strong, emotionally charged facade of polite humility, hospitality, goodwill and cooperativeness. Westerners who are unfamiliar with this multi-leveled combination of cultural forms tend to be confused and frustrated when they are confronted with them as a concentrated force.

The Japanese approach to consensus building is a vital part of their negotiating technique and, planned or not, is often a significant part of their business tactics. This kata-ized approach requires that the matter at hand be broken down into its smallest possible facets or units, and that each of these bits be meticulously scrutinized from every angle to make sure everyone in the group totally understands the subject and has every piece of information that might be relevant.

This microscopic approach—reflective of training in Kan-Ji—naturally takes time and demands a level of research and response that the typical Westerner regards as overkill, and often not worth the time, energy or cost. To the Japanese, however, persevering and taking things a small slice at a time is the name of the game. Foreign businessmen, whether stationed in Japan or on a visit, who attempt to circumvent this deeply embedded pattern of behavior—by giving orders, holding a one-hour briefing session and setting a deadline, etc.—are invariably frustrated when nothing happens or things go awry.

Generally speaking, there is no way for the foreign businessman to avoid this standard Japanese negotiating practice if he is the one seeking to deal with the Japanese. In that case, the best recourse is to learn how the system works and how to operate within it—which often means hiring a good Japanese negotiator who is conditioned to split infinite hairs and will do so on your behalf.

Interestingly, by the late 1970s many Japanese companies had begun a practice of hiring foreigners to teach them how to deal with foreigners.

TRAVELING BY THE NUMBERS

Japan's awesomely efficient tourist industry is a very conspicuous example of their dedication to detail, form and process. One of the most common sights in Tokyo as well as other major cities and sightseeing destinations are groups of Japanese students, farmers and members of various associations moving about in orderly masses.

Such tours are scripted down to the last detail, including taking the groups to pre-arranged stores to do their mandatory shopping for the *mei butsu* (may-e boot-sue) or "famous products" of the area. At restaurants everyone typically eats the same thing. An American teacher who accompanied three thousand high school students on one of their annual outings said, "I don't think they (the teachers) allowed for one spontaneous second. Everything was organized ..."

Often, especially in the case of young students, the groups will be dressed exactly the same. They are especially conspicuous when it is raining and all are wearing yellow or orange raincoats and rain hats.

This sightseeing kata goes back nearly four hundred years and is a natural outgrowth of the Japanese way of doing things in a highly organized manner for the sake of efficiency as well as order. Systematic recreational travel in Japan began in the mid-1600s when religious groups called *ko* began organizing tours to distant temples and shrines as pilgrimages. Local neighborhood and shrine groups were formed for each major destination—Nikko Ko, Ise Ko, and so on.

These religious pilgrims traveled on foot, as did all other common people in Japan, and were thus on the road for weeks at a time when going to distant destinations. They moved in programmed formations that were as meticulously structured as military units on the march, following the dictates of cultural conditioning that had already been going on for centuries and was to continue down to contemporary times.

Even more conspicuous/ and certainly far more important culturally, politically and economically, were the great "Processions of Lords" that were an extraordinary part of Japanese life for over two hundred years. This phenomenon began in the late 1630s when the ruling Tokugawa Shogun decreed that some 270 of the country's clan lords would maintain residences in Edo (present-day Tokyo), keep their wives and children there at all times as hostages, and themselves alternately spend every other three years in Edo to attend the Shogun's Court.

This law, designed to keep the clan lords under control and to prevent them from building up a strong economic base that might threaten the shogunate, specified how many warriors and retainers each lord would bring with him on his trips to the capital, how they would be dressed, their behavior and the routes they were to take. The procession of the Maeda, the largest and richest of the clans, consisted of more than a thousand people.

For generation after generation, these great, colorful processions passed to and fro on Japan's roadways, demonstrating the power of the local lord and the ruling Tokugawa family, as well as carrying culture and homogenizing the nation.

Remnants of such mass conditioning, still visible in such ordinary pursuits as recreational traveling, are yet another measure of the vital nature of the kata factor in everyday life in Japan—now also witnessed daily in countries around the world among the millions of Japanese who annually travel abroad to shop, visit world-famous landmarks and honeymoon.

RECONFIRMING JAPANESENESS

My own favorite Japanese kata in action is a formalized banquet party called an *enkai* (en-kie), which is one of the most common and popular events in Japan. Participants in enkai parties are members of specific groups from companies, associations, agencies, schools, etc. The parties are held at Japanese-style restaurants, inns, hotels, large banquet halls, and at hot spring spas.

Enkai banquets are perfect examples of Japan's kata-driven and homogenized group culture. Everything is carefully and meticulously carried out according to well-practiced custom—the seating, food, service and entertainment follow a traditional format that goes back for centuries.

When the banquet party takes place at a hot springs inn—Japan has over two thousand hot spring spas—participants are often dressed in identical cotton yukata (yuu-kaha-tah) robes provided by the inn. The entire program is orchestrated by a *kanji* (kahn-jee) or tour captain and followed by the numbers. Everything that is done reinforces the group orientation, mutual dependence and cooperative spirit of the group.

It is necessary to be emotionally, spiritually and intellectually tuned to the Japanese Way to fully appreciate the meaning and importance of the enkai to the Japanese. Enkai are one of the primary "soul springs" of the Japanese, essential to their well-being in the deepest cultural sense. I have participated in hundreds of these cultural rituals and can attest to their spiritual and emotional impact, and to their effects in reaffirming the validity of the Japanese Way and their group maintenance magic.

Virtually every adult Japanese who is well enough to get out of his house attends at least one enkai a year. Many, especially businessmen and professionals, typically attend one or more banquet parties each month. It is possible that the outsider who is not versed well enough in the Japanese language and customs to fully join in the ritual of the enkai, or similar Japanese rituals, is forever barred from an important level of intimacy with Japan.

Enkai parties are a microcosm of Japanese culture in action, far more important to an understanding and appreciation of the Japanese Way than the aesthetic arts which Japan generally emphasizes to foreign visitors and tries to export.

BASEBALL THE WA WAY

Not surprisingly, there is a kata for baseball as it is played in Japan. As the Japanese characteristically do with most things they import, they have Japanized the game to suit the national mind-set—much to the dismay of many American athletes who have played the game in Japan—and in the process made it into a topic that has inspired two of the more entertaining and insightful books on Japan in recent years: *The Chrysanthemum and the Bat* and *You Gotta Have Wa*, both by Robert Whiting.

How the Japanese play professional baseball is one of the best examples of their process and group orientation. On a Japanese baseball team it is not how well you play, but how well you train and *how* you play that is important—a factor that totally mystifies and eventually frustrates most American athletes who hire out to Japanese baseball clubs.

On the one hand, American players are hired by Japanese ball clubs for their hitting or pitching prowess. But the Americans may find themselves in a double bind if they do too well. If they show up their own teammates *or* the players on the opposing team, they may be deliberately handicapped to make it more difficult—or impossible—for them to perform as well.

Among the handicaps that have been applied to foreign baseball players to control their performance: taking them out of the line-up when they are having a hitting streak; enlarging the strike zone so pitches that would normally be balls become strikes (without telling the batter of the new temporary rule), and replacing a pitcher who is striking out too many players.

The very "Japanese" point that most foreign baseball players cannot appreciate was that they were expected to produce on cue when there was no danger of anyone losing face. If they failed to produce when expected or do more than is expected, they were in trouble.

Another aspect of Japanese *besuboru* (bay-sue-boe-rue) is the extraordinary emphasis on training, physical and mental, required by the managers and coaches. It goes so far beyond what American players consider necessary or desirable that they regard it as irrational.

What is often even more disturbing to American players on Japanese baseball teams is the degree of togetherness and team harmony that is required. The whole team is expected to behave as a single-cell unit. The individualism and idiosyncrasies for which American players are famous are strictly taboo.

Another point that imported American baseball players generally missed was that in Japan baseball was less of a game that is played for fun and more of a medium for developing and demonstrating spirit and harmony. In Japan, spirit, dedication and discipline have much higher priorities than recreation and creativity.

No matter how skilled or how high the repute (or the salary) of the newly arrived American baseball player, the first thing the Japanese managers and coaches attempted to do was to make him over in their image. Their conditioning in the kata of baseball was so strong that their instructions to the new foreign batting ace may include how he was supposed to hold his bat.

This same obsession with form and process is repeated endlessly in every area of private and public life in Japan. It often works beautifully where automation and assembly lines are concerned, but when human interaction is involved it often requires an extraordinary emotional investment, slows things down and complicates matters.

COPYING AS A NATIONAL SKILL

From about 1870 until 1970 the Japanese were often roundly criticized as copiers instead of innovators. They were, in fact, geniuses at copying. But rather than this being a fault, their skill at imitating and adapting foreign customs and technology has proven to be one of their greatest strengths.

It was Japanese skill in copying, among other factors, that made it possible for Japan to become the technology-based economic power it is today. Here again it was centuries of accumulated knowledge and experience, primarily gained through kata, that gave the Japanese an edge in becoming consummate copiers.

It took the Japanese a while to develop the confidence to make improvements in the things they copied. Some of the

Western products they duplicated for their own use prior to the downfall of the feudal shogunate in 1868 were faithful reproductions, including the design failings as well as the primitive workmanship. Again as already mentioned, during most of the century that they were derisively described as copiers practically all of the things they copied were done on order from foreign importers who, in most cases, were not interested in high quality products.

Now, in addition to wholesale copying, Japanese are among the world's most successful inventors and innovators because of their kata-oriented cultural skills and the added factor that the ultimate goal of all their traditional kata is step-by-step improvement until total mastery is achieved—an attitude that remains very much in evidence today and is summed up in the key word *kai zen* (kie-zen), which means "continuous improvement."

DRESSING THE JAPANESE PSYCHE

During several periods of Japan's feudal age, wearing apparel was generally prescribed by law, and what was not legally mandated was controlled by rigid custom. There was a prescribed dress for members of the royal court, the shogun and his court, the samurai class, for merchants and other commoners. The date when people changed from summer to winter attire and vice-versa was officially announced—and was often at considerable variance with the weather.

The codifying of wearing apparel, based on class and occupation, was institutionalized to the point that wearing the wrong kind of apparel was a serious offense. Not only were the specific items of clothing prescribed for each group, the way clothing was put on, worn and taken off, was kata-ized.

Centuries of conditioning in the right kind of clothing

and in the style of wearing it made the Japanese extra-ordinarily sensitive to apparel, its style, color and quality—a sensitivity that remains an important part of the mentality and consciousness of present-day Japanese.

This attitude toward clothing carries over into all kinds of apparel, from business suits to sportswear. The kata for dressing combines with the kata of practicing or playing tennis or golf or whatever, making it virtually mandatory that the person dress "right" for the game, meaning the "right" clothing as well as the "right" equipment.

Skiers who are on the slopes for the first time do not feel right unless they are dressed like professionals and sporting brand-name equipment. First-time tennis players want to look exactly like the world-famous stars who play before the cameras at Wimbledon.

Merchandisers of wearing apparel in general and sports-wear in particular, along with sports equipment suppliers, have taken full advantage of these cultural factors in their marketing in Japan.

CUTENESS AND INFANTILISM

There is a shikata for feminine cuteness in Japan. This traditional cuteness kata consists of girls and young women simulating baby-like gestures and speech in a type of behavior that is highly prized by Japanese men as portraying innocence and virginal sexuality. Such contrived baby cuteness is a common practice among cabaret hostesses, is seen regularly in television commercials, and is carefully fostered in Japan's legends of teenage girl TV singers, known as "idol singers."

"Idol singers" refers to a phenomenon that began in Japan in the 1960s as a result of the overwhelming popularity of American music among young people. Because quality Western style musicians and singers were still rare, the burgeoning new television industry began creating entertainment stars virtually overnight to help attract viewers. The primary focus of this effort was the systematic selection of rather cute girls in their early teens who were then put through a rigorous kata-ized process to teach them a specifically choreographed form to follow while singing and interacting with the audience.

Standard choreography for each of the teenage singers consisted of a few dance-like steps and a series of simple hand movements, all of which were repeated endlessly during performances. The instant TV stars looked and acted like cute little wound-up dolls. Many of them were particularly conspicuous to foreign viewers because they had one or more overlapping teeth—traditionally regarded by the Japanese as a beauty mark, perhaps because it was so common.

Few of the thirteen- and fourteen-year-old girls had really good voices and most were poor singers, but that was not the point. They were selected and packaged to represent role models, or "idols," for the millions of teenagers who were targeted as customers for their concerts and recordings.

Packagers of idol singers knew exactly what they were doing. The system became a huge success, and continues today. There is a fresh crop of "new faces" each year, with most of the "older" girls going back to ordinary careers as high school students and later company employees—their bloom of virginal freshness gone by the time they are seventeen.

In Japan an infantile-cute kind of behavior has also been traditionally sanctioned for men in their relations with women, particularly in the night-time entertainment trades. In most instances when men go into the infantile mode, women automatically adopt a mothering role, whether the expected response is tender, loving care, or sex.

This cultural role-playing of infantile innocence by young Japanese women and Japanese men of any age is very conspicuous to Westerners who tend to see it in a very negative sense. It is one of the reasons why Westerners have traditionally underestimated the sophistication, maturity and ability of the Japanese.

THE SHIKATA OF BEING JAPANESE

A sense of uniqueness continues to permeate the Japanese. They feel different not only because of their historical isolation and the protective barrier presented by their language, but also because enough of their kata-ized culture remains to set them apart in a variety of measureable ways.

Inroads made by Western (primarily American) culture on Japan, and the notion gaining ground among the Japanese that they must "internationalize" (become less Japanese) in order to stay on good terms with the world, presents the Japanese with a dilemma that has divided the country into two camps—those who want to hold onto their traditional uniqueness, and those, still in the minority, who are making a genuine effort to adopt more Western ways of viewing and doing things.

However, most of those who do appreciate the Western mind-set, and understand how and when it is advantageous, are not so blinded that they renounce the culture of Japan out of hand. Most are quick to point out that the Japanese system remains superior in many ways.

Competition between the Japanese and Western systems is fierce and often results in contradictions and conflicts among the Japanese. Many often have two personalities—a traditional Japanese personality and a Western personality. Some are practiced enough to easily slip from one to the other as the occasion demands, but many such people readily admit that functioning in their Western personality is a serious strain that can leave them exhausted.

Extended exposure to Western culture also generally "taints" the Japanese to the extent that they have extreme difficulty reverting back to their Japanese character. Some become so Westernized they simply cannot change back. In the more traditional business and professional fields, they are often shut out completely because the kata-ized Japanese Way demands virtually absolute exclusivity.

Foreigners who saw the growing number of Westernized Japanese as catalysts for the internationalization of the country were in for a long wait. Despite their growing numbers, most of these people remained outside of the pale, isolated in their own never-never land. What they wrote and said, usually in English, generally went no farther than their foreign audience.

Interestingly, the Japanese are far more susceptible to Westernization than foreigners are to Japanization. Two or three years of living abroad is often enough to Westernize a Japanese to a considerable degree. Foreigners often live in Japan for twenty or thirty years without any noticeable Japanization of their character or personality.

There are no doubt a number of reasons for the Westerner's immunity to Japanization. The kata culture of Japan is too intricate, subtle, demanding, and groupistic to be appealing to most foreigners. The system was also so exclusive that generally outsiders were not accepted under any circumstances, and the few foreigners who did make a serious effort to become "Japanese" were rebuffed.

Many Japanese companies that assigned staff overseas went to extraordinary lengths to help them maintain their Japaneseness while abroad. This includes a massive amount of communication, far beyond that necessary for strictly business purposes. Some made frequent trips home that were more to sustain personal relations with their colleagues than to conduct business.

Until the late 1980s, part of the kata of being Japanese was an almost universal belief in the idea that entry into the Japanese market by foreign companies should be tightly controlled and limited, irrespective of any benefits to the Japanese consumer or any obligations of reciprocity the Japanese might have for the right to sell their own products abroad.

In the past, opposition to foreign-made products entering the Japanese market traditionally took a variety of practiced forms. The government or company involved generally would not oppose a specific product directly. One typical ploy was to delay things by asking questions, by doing more "testing" or "studying"—while in the meantime they were sometimes gearing up to produce whatever product was concerned in Japan. There are still cases where larger Japanese companies as well as government agencies and ministries also systematically bring pressure against Japanese distributors and suppliers to prevent them from cooperating with foreign firms.

Another ploy that allegedly has been common among large Japanese companies was to contract with foreign companies in similar or related lines of business to distribute their products in Japan, then severely limit the distribution to prevent the products from become serious competition.

Japanese today have overcome this anti-foreign product syndrome, but the majority continue to believe that foreign products in general are not suitable for the Japanese market until they have been properly Japanized. This feeling goes beyond anything having to do with size, design or quality. It is an innate symptom that goes back to the exclusivity of their kata-ized culture—and serves them well in their efforts to "protect" the Japanese marketplace.

BEHIND THE BAMBOO CURTAIN

There is no great mystery behind the symbols that conceal Japan from the outside world—or for that matter, prevent the Japanese from seeing the outside world as it actually is. Kurt Singer, an educator-economist who lived in Japan in the 1930s, is one of many who have noted that the Japanese are hard to understand not because they are complicated, but because they are so simple.

Of course, Singer and these other observers go on to qualify what they mean by simple. In this case they are referring to the fact that the Japanese accept as normal contradictions and chaos that other people consider irrational if not mad. They go on to say that the Japanese do not meet conflicts head on and fight them, they avoid them, by compromise or by ignoring them. They add that characteristically in Japan, it is more important to avoid conflicts than to eliminate evil.

Public behavior in Japan, which is usually all the foreign viewer can see or understand, is designed to maintain harmony and allow time for things to be worked out behind the scenes. Things that cannot be quickly or easily resolved by consensus are usually tolerated until they change or die of their own accord.

In the same way, the lack of form and disorder that the Japanese perceive in the thinking and behavior of Americans and other Westerners is seen as a cultural and personal failing. It is also one of the key reasons why the Japanese consider themselves inherently superior to foreigners.

DEALING WITH FOREIGNERS

Historically the Japanese were unable to accept non-Japanese into their society. This intolerance went beyond both race and language. Persons of Korean or Chinese ancestry who are physically identical to the Japanese and whose families had lived in Japan for generations and were totally assimilated into the culture were not accepted as Japanese.

The non-Oriental person living in Japan, citizen or not, was naturally more alien than Oriental persons of non-Japanese ancestry. The idea of Caucasians, Blacks and other races becoming "Japanese" was unthinkable. The most ever accorded to them was Japanese citizenship.

As a result of such cultural discrimination, the Japanese developed specific ways of dealing with foreigners, depending on circumstances and the category of the foreigners involved. These ways consisted of attitudes and kata for dealing with foreign diplomats and politicians, businessmen, tourists, students and residents. Regardless of the circumstance or who was involved, the fundamental factor was that the relationship involved a non-Japanese.

In the Japanese scheme of things a foreigner was a non-Japanese first, an individual second, and possibly a business associate third. This subtle discrimination permeated Japanese thinking and behavior, some of it subconsciously and some of it deliberately contrived. The Japanese claimed that they did not discriminate against anyone. Their position was that they treated other Japanese one way and everyone else another way—and did not recognize this dichotomy as discrimination.

Japanese did not see themselves as anti-foreigner in the usual sense of the term. To strain an analogy, they saw themselves as apples and other people as oranges. To them, keeping the two apart was just common sense. "To be regarded as and treated as a Japanese you have to be born in Japan, of Japanese parents, and raised as a Japanese in the full cultural implications of the word," says Japanologist Ken Butler. It is necessary to add to this that the candidate for full Japanese-hood must also *not* be a member of Japan's own Japanese minority caste *(burakumin)* whose ancestors slaughtered animals and worked with hides—which was used for armor.

Few Caucasian residents of Japan complained very much about being excluded from Japanese society. Author Donald Richie, one of the most perceptive observers of the Japanese scene, summed up the situation succinctly in an interview published *in Japan As We Lived It: Can East and West Ever Meet,* by Bernard Krishner (Yohan Publications, Tokyo). Richie stated that if he were a Japanese he wouldn't stay in Japan for ten minutes. "The weight of (the) society on a person who is Japanese is very heavy," he said. The truth of the matter is life in Japan was only tolerable for most Caucasian residents *because* they were excluded from the society and treated differently.

Japanese have traditionally had separate policies and rules for dealing with foreigners, all originally designed to prevent foreign penetration into Japan or to minimize it and keep it under control. These policies and rules naturally were aimed at protecting Japan's interests—political, social and economic—and had nothing to do with fairness or reciprocity.

While generalizations about the Japanese kata for treating foreigners are open to individual interpretation, there are some instances when it is obvious and undeniable. Probably the most conspicuous example, mentioned earlier, was Japanese attitudes toward foreign tourists and their traditional treatment of them. As short-term visitors who are in Japan to enjoy the beauty of the islands and indulge in some of the attractions of the culture, travelers present neither a threat nor a challenge to the Japanese.

This so-called "guest culture" incorporates an elaborate body of kata for the care and feeding of guests that keeps them impressed and happy for the most part, but also has the effect of isolating them from the realities of Japan.

Tourists are, of course, looked upon as guests of the country. The Japanese are past masters at providing a regal level of service to guests, believing that if the guests fail to enjoy themselves and to go home enormously impressed with Japan, all Japanese have lost face. Foreign visitors who are recipients of typical Japanese hospitality are often tremendously impressed and become great fans of the whole country.

In earlier times encounters with all other non-tourist categories of foreigners caused the Japanese varying degrees of consternation. In the first place, communication was almost always incomplete and often nil because of the language barrier. In the second place, cultural differences in values, motivations and methods invariably resulted in further gaps in understanding. Traditional fears and pre-judices often intensify these factors.

One of the manifestations of Japanese distrust of non-tourist foreigners was a lingering innate suspicion of all foreigners who had more than a casual interest in Japan. This feeling was a holdover from the long era when every foreigner in Japan was believed to be in the country for ulterior and eventually harmful motives. Japanese were generally unable to give a foreign resident, student, businessman or official the benefit of the doubt. He or she had to prove himself or herself as friendly and trustworthy on a regular basis, from the first meeting on.

Proof of friendship and trustworthiness expected from foreigners by many Japanese, particularly those who weree traditionally oriented, entailed a kind and degree of behavior that often smacked of flattery, if not toadyism. Interestingly, many foreigners were so eager to impress and please the Japanese, for one reason or another, that they went overboard in their praise and actions even when it wasn't expected or necessary.

This latter type of behavior was likely to come across as insincere, reflecting badly on the foreigner and constituting yet another barrier to understanding and goodwill.

On the surface it would seem that foreigners who speak Japanese and are practiced in behaving "in Japanese style" would be the least likely to create special problems for the Japanese and have the most success in functioning effectively in Japan.

This generally appears to be so in strictly social matters, but in business it is often not the case. The experience of one of my life-long friends is typical. After substantial "Asian" experience in Korea and Taiwan, he arrived in Tokyo in the early 1950s, determined not to fall into the familiar pattern of becoming either a hardcore Japanophile or Japanophobe. His story:

"I dedicated myself to disproving the theory that all *gaijin* (guy-jeen)—foreigners—in Japan *had* to either love the country or hate it. I set out to relate to Japan on the basis of total objectivity, and to do that by becoming totally fluent in the language, structuring my business and social life within the pure Japanese context and studying firsthand every aspect of the Japanese way of doing things.

"I pursued my program of total immersion for three decades. Japanism was my thing. No Kan-Ji escaped by every-ready notebook. The kata for any occasion, including hospital visits and funerals, became a knee-jerk reaction. I could lead business meetings in the Japanese language. I was as comfortable on the reed-mat floor of a Yanagibashi geisha inn as I was at Keen's Chop House in New York. I believed I was the optimum 'good' gaijin. I was certain that I had disproved the conventional wisdom of the old Japan hands which said that no foreigner, including third-generation 'born-again' Koreans—was ever accepted in Japan. I was frequently interviewed by the media about my experiences in Japan, and asked to write and speak about the country by prestigious organizations.

"*I* felt that I had reached the point that I could be both American and Japanese—I believed that I had crossed the 'gaijin line;' that I was accepted in both societies on an equal basis. Given this mind-set, I established a joint venture with a major Japanese company with whom I had already been doing business for several years as a supplier. The idea was to maximize the potential of the patented technology my company had acquired. My firm owned 45 percent of the joint venture; the much larger Japanese company owned 55 percent.

"I became the director of international operations in the new joint venture, and my long-time friend and drinking buddy from the Japanese side became the managing director. I was immediately relegated to observer status. 1 was never asked to attend any management meetings. I tried everything I had learned about the Japanese way of doing business—the ringi (formal proposal documents), nemawashi (informal lobbying), nomination (drinking together in bars)—the gamut of culturally sanctioned practices. I brought in new ideas and new products. Everybody was polite and accommodating, but I was otherwise totally ignored.

"The new joint venture became extremely profitable, so in that sense I could not fault the Japanese side. But I was angered and frustrated that after more than thirty years of business experience in Japan I was not accepted as a team member in a company in which I was a near equal owner. The awful truth came slowly; painfully. The old Japan hands had been right all along. Everything was fine as long as I was content to stay on the outside and be treated as a guest.

"With this realization came an understanding of the gaijin proclivity for becoming Japanophobes or Japanophiles. The Japanophiles—often those who have not become deeply enough involved in the culture to learn that they can never be accepted—may be the lucky ones. The Japanese have kata for dealing with foreigners on the fringes of their society but not accepting them within their inner circle."

This old friend divided the Japanese kata for dealing with foreigners into three distinct categories: *gaijin no tori-atsukae kata* (guy-jeen no toe-ree-aht-sue-kie kah-tah)—how to handle, treat and deal with foreigners in business situations; *gaijin no atsukae kata* (guy-jeen no aht-sue-kie kah-tah)—how to handle foreigners in day-to-day arm's length relationships; and *gaijin no tsukiau kata* (guy-jeen no t'sue-kee-ow kah-tah)—how to relate socially to foreigners at parties and public functions.

He added: "Anyone considering any sort of commitment to Japan should be aware of these fundamental kata and the closed nature of the society, and expect to be treated accordingly."

Foreign women in management positions in Japan often presented a special problem for Japanese businessmen, who generally had no experience in treating women as equals, much less as superiors. It was particularly difficult for such men to deal directly with foreign female managers because virtually none of the hallowed ways men in Japan communicate and commune with each other—using rough language, visiting cabarets and geisha inns, playing golf as an extension of business relationships—were considered appropriate for women. The younger the foreign businesswoman in Japan the more likely she was to upset the kata-ized equilibrium of older male Japanese counterparts.

A young Canadian businesswoman, who spoke very good Japanese and was a department manager in a major American corporation in Tokyo, said she found that un-Westernized Japanese businessmen had no idea how to treat her. She said that when she took a younger, junior Japanese employee with her to meetings these businessmen would direct all of their conversation to the Japanese person, ignoring the fact that the junior employee referred all questions and decisions to her in Japanese and she responded in that language.

This same young foreign woman, who had majored in Asian studies and the Japanese language and spent time in Japan on a scholarship prior to going to work in Tokyo, recalled her earlier attempts to integrate into Japanese society. "When I came to Japan as a student I lived with a Japanese family, spoke only Japanese, went by a Japanese name and learned all of the etiquette and special expressions that are a part of daily life. But at the end of a year I was still as much of an outsider as I had been on my first day. 'My God,' I said, 'it isn't happening!'"

Because ordinary Japanese typically has trouble

accepting bilingual, bicultural foreigners whom they had come to know and like, they often went to extremes in trying to explain the situation. Sometimes their attempts to rationalize how a foreigner could come to know and use their culture were bizarre. One of the more common rationalizations was that the foreigner was actually Japanese despite his appearance. If this self-induced illusion was shattered they were disturbed.

It wass also characteristic of the Japanese to refer to foreigners who knew Japan well as *wakarisugiru* (wah-kah-ree-suu-ghee-ree) or as "knowing too much." The term was frequently used in a friendly or joking manner, but it nevertheless expressed the built-in fear the Japanese had of being exposed or becoming understandable to outsiders.

Japanese requirements for continuously proving one's loyalty and commitment to Japan wa not limited to foreigners. The Japanese themselves must constantly reaffirm their Japaneseness in numerous ways—by following certain customs, eating certain foods, taking acceptable positions on issues, and so on. This reaffirmation is both private and public and is part of the Japanese process of maintaining their identity and mental health.

One of the most controversial issues facing Japan today is the way they treat foreign residents, especially those who have migrated to the country illegally to find jobs. I was among the first few foreigners to be hired full-time—but not as regular employees with benefits—by Japanese companies following the end of World War II. By the mid-1950s several hundred English-speaking foreigners had been engaged by Japanese firms on a temporary basis, primarily as English teachers, writers and editors.

This pattern was to continue for the next two decades or so, by which time there was growing pressure both internally and externally for Japanese companies to at least make a token move toward liberalizing their employment practices. The growing internationalization of business in Japan—on the manufacturing, retailing and exporting levels—made it increasingly obvious that many Japanese companies could clearly benefit from having some foreign employees.

At the same time, negative publicity about Japan's closed-door employment policies in the international media began to detract from the country's image abroad—a factor that generally is far more important to the Japanese than any disadvantages they might suffer from not employing foreign staff. These and other factors combined have resulted in a growing number of Japanese firms employing one or more foreigners, sometimes in key positions, but more often on a token basis.

Given the built-in ethnocentricity of the Japanese culture, combined with very realistic political and social con- siderations, it is unlikely that Japan will ever open its employment doors more than a hairline crack to expatriate foreign workers. In a typical but strained effort to downplay the natural Japanese antipathy toward expatriate foreign workers in Japan, the news media in recent years has noted that descendants of Japanese who emigrated to Brazil are welcome despite the fact that they usually cannot speak Japanese and are not familiar with the Japanese way of doing things.

Japanese-Americans who returned to Japan in small but significant numbers after the end of World War II were not welcomed with open arms by corporate Japan. They were been treated as curiosities, to be kept at arm's length. Japanese Brazilians who showed up in Japan received the same kind of treatment.

One of the several reasons given by the Japanese for not

routinely hiring foreigners who have skills they need was that since foreigners generally do not know and cannot follow the Japanese Way, they are unpredictable and would cause more problems than they would solve. Interestingly, this excuse was rapidly losing its justification, however, as more and more of the foreigners seeking white-collar work in Japan did speak Japanese and wew familiar with the culture.

The close-knittedness and security provided by Japan's web of kata made the Japanese exquisitely sensitive to anything unexpected. They could not stand for things to be unpredictable—which was one of the reasons why those who were un-Westernized were so uncomfortable when dealing with foreigners. Because they could not predict what foreigners were going to say or do, such Japanese were under constant stress when in their presence.

These factors were often further complicated when some older Japanese wewre concerned because they took special pride in their Japaneseness and worked very hard at it, sometimes to the extent that their pride and prejudices outran their common sense. Naturally enough, these people were the most difficult for Westerners to understand and deal with.

One life-long foreign resident of Japan said the Japanese habitually retreated into ceremonious formality when they faced any unfamiliar situation, and that ceremony is also used as an escape from reality. "Kata have, in fact, traditionally been used to replace honest human relationships," he said.

The same observer added that the social etiquette the Japanese developed to support the shikata system doesn't fit in the modern world, but that without kata the Japanese were lost and did not know how to behave. "From a Western viewpoint the Japanese had been dehumanized by their dependence on kata/' he added.

KATA IN POLITICS

Not surprisingly, the form and order of Japanese politics follows traditional patterns of behavior, meaning that the system is based on groupings (factions) rather than true party lines or clear political principles; members of these individual groups are arranged in a hierarchical order; seniority and longevity generally take precedence over character and talent; and decisions are based on a consensus within the factions or among them when the cooperation of other factions is necessary.

The largest and strongest of the factions tend to monopolize the positions of privilege and power, but very little authority is invested in individuals or in offices. Government policy-making on both a national and pre-fectural level is more or less a group effort with several groups contending against each other, while the day-to-day administration of the prefectures and national affairs is left to bureaucrats.

This system obviously works well enough within the Japanese context of things that it—along with the whole culture—has survived for a long time. But it ranges from only partly effective to hopeless when trying to deal with international affairs because there is no central locus of power and the foreign side is unable to deal with it effectively.

At the end of the 1980s a series of scandals involving ranking politicians and businessmen resulted in a national outcry for a reformation of the Japanese political system. Any real change in the system will, of course, have to evolve along with the changing culture over a long period of time.

Some of the formulas used by Japan's Foreign Office in its relations with the American Embassy in Tokyo were indicative of how the culture was manipulated to benefit the Japanese. Virtually all of the Foreign Office personnel directly involved with the U.S. spoke good or passable English. The Japanese made sure that the joint study programs sponsored by the embassy and Foreign Office were conducted in English. Practically all of the informal conversations between Foreign Office and Embassy personnel at the continuous round of parties are also in English.

This makes it possible for Japanese diplomats to say what the foreign side likes to hear, but to keep their comments completely divorced from the reality of the Japanese attitude and position when it serves their purpose. Part of the psychology is that whatever they say in English doesn't count. The same psychology generally applies in all situations. Bilingual Japanese regularly say and write all kinds of things in English and other foreign languages that they wouldn't dare express in Japanese.

By the same token they customarily express opinions in Japanese that are strictly for Japanese consumption, and tend to become very upset when such comments are published in other languages. Interestingly, the Japanese generally do not see anything immoral or unprincipled in basing their comments and behavior on the language they are speaking. Many readily admit that such duplicity is necessary because the Japanese side would not understand or would get angry— or in other cases, because the foreign side would react in an undesirable way.

The factor at play in this situation is that the Japanese perceive their own reality as differing from foreign reality, that each is in its own dimension, and that mixing the two is either uncalled for or dangerous. They are able to consistently control most meetings with their foreign counterparts because the foreign side usually does not speak

Japanese well enough to communicate fully in the language and either accepts what the Japanese say or remains frustrated.

One of the most blatant barriers used in Japan to keep foreigners away from the inner workings of politics and the economy are the notorious "press clubs" which traditionally barred foreign journalists from having equal access to news sources. Each of the key news sources in the country, from the prime minister's office to major corporations, has a press club made up of selected members of the Japanese press. Foreign journalists could not join the clubs and until the 1980s could not attend press conferences arranged by the clubs or the news sources—unless they were separate meetings arranged especially for foreign newsmen.

The Japanese rationale for barring foreign reporters from their press conferences was simple. They said the sessions were conducted in Japanese which few if any of the foreign journalists could speak; foreign journalists would most likely misunderstand the statements and policies of the business and government spokesmen because their comments were made for a Japanese audience; since foreigners did not understand the Japanese way of doing things the journalists could not accurately report on the proceedings and would create problems between Japan and the world at large, and so on.

It took nearly forty years of pressure, and fundamental changes in Japan's culture, before this extraordinary barrier was even partially breached.

THE LAYERED CULTURE

In the Japanese scheme of things, as already mentioned, aesthetic values, harmony and maintenance of the correct order of things can take precedence over what the West tends to regard as ethical and moral principles. This concept underpins many of the political and business policies followed by Japan today that Westerners view as irrational.

The built-in need for avoiding disruptions of any kind is also partly responsible for the Japanese habit of importing foreign ideas and things, categorizing them and keeping them separate from traditional Japan. This approach has allowed them to graft layers of foreign culture onto their own without losing their own distinctive ways.

Japan has never imported Western technology with the idea of changing its system to be more like that of the West. Its importation of Western knowhow was first based on the concept of protecting Japan from inroads by foreign powers, and then, later, on continuing to enhance its competitive position on the international scene.

Despite Japan's copious borrowings from Korea and China in the past and the advanced Western nations today, once the Japanese have imported an idea, a custom or a product, they transform it into something that is different, with a certain Japaneseness that is always present. No sensitive person can spend more than a few days in Japan without realizing that Japanese culture has a style and a sense of its own that is a significant factor in the strength of the country.

Foreigners can live a lifetime in Japan, however, and not fully understand how the Japanese system works as well as it does. Japanese culture, unlike much of American culture, is not always open and visible, and does not travel well. At the same time, Japanese culture can be easily discarded in a short period of time, while Western culture is difficult to shed. Life within the core of Japanese society is indeed like a silken web, often times incandescently beautiful to the outsider, but bonds of steel to those caught up in it.

Most of Japan's perceived internationalization or Westernization is a facade that touches the skin of older people but does not penetrate it. They may dress Western and eat Western, and occasionally behave Western, but for the most part they continue to think and act in a distinctively Japanese manner. They are very sensitive about these differences and comment on them constantly.

In the past theJapanese automatically expressed wonder when a foreigner demonstrated even the smallest "Japanese-like" skill, whether it was the Japanese language or the use of chopsticks. Their reaction was an instinctive, kata-ized response that eventually became very irritating to long-time foreign residents, especially to those who spoke the language well and had been using chopsticks routinely for several decades. Said one: "It makes me feel like a trick monkey."

This stereotypical reaction of the Japanese was another reason why many foreigners have traditionally regarded them as intellectually inferior.

There are many daily examples of the extraordinary hold that traditional Japanese culture continues to have on the average person. One of the most telling is when they demonstrate an innate inability to accept even the slightest, invisible differences between a "true" Japanese and anyone who has been touched by some aspect of non-Japanese influence.

When Japan was forcibly opened to commerce with the West in the 1850s by the U.S., the Japanese very quickly made a clear distinction between what they wanted to import from the West and what they wanted to avoid. They saw themselves as far more cultured than Westerners and far superior in spirit, but seriously lacking in academic and technological knowledge.

They immediately began a massive program of bringing in foreign educators and technicians to help them industrialize their economic infrastructure—a stupendous feat that was accomplished in less than twenty years in large part because of their spirit and kata conditioning—and a feat that they were to repeat between 1945 and I960, the period when they rebuilt their economy from the ashes of World War II, again with the massive use of foreign technology and knowhow.

BECOMING INTERNATIONAL

Japanese are acutely aw^are that their economic success is based on maintaining friendly, cooperative relations with the U.S. and Europe. They are even more aware of the cultural chasm that separates them from the West. In a broad sense they realize they must change their way of thinking and doing things in order to keep political and trade friction within manageable levels. In addition to this economic and political pressure to change, there is also growing social pressure emanating from those who were born after 1960 and have not been fully Japanized.

These combined factors resulted in a movement that is generally referred to as *kokusai-ka* (koke-sie-kah) or "internationalization," which was a catch-all phrase covering any move away from traditional Japanese attitudes, behavior and styles. The first stages stage of the movement were more style and form than substance. But among the young in particular the desire was real enough and they spent enormous amounts of money and time engaging in "international" activities that range from studying English, traveling abroad and eating Western style foods to shopping in exclusive boutiques.

114

Clashes between the old way and the new "international" way are constantly recurring themes throughout Japanese society. What has emerged is a new Japan that is a long way from the old, but it will not Western either.

4
KATA IN BUSINESS
LEARNING THE ROLES & RULES

Knowledge of kata that apply in business and professional relationships in modern-day Japan, along with skill in using them and being able to predict their effects, is especially critical for Japanese as well as foreigners because it is in the business and professional worlds that the kata culture is the strongest. Key kata in these areas, more or less in the order in which they come into play, include the following:

Aisatsu no shikata (Aye-sot-sue no she-kah-tah)

This is the formal Japanese or way of greeting or acknowledging other people. Aisatsu by itself is usually translated as greeting, but when used in its full form it covers an abundance of important social etiquette, from using third parties as go-betweens, bowing and exchanging name-cards to using the right level of language at the right time.

The initial aisatsu as well as subsequent behavior is directly influenced by your own perceived status in the sense of social class and business or professional rank, age and so on. These factors play a role concerning whom you qualify to meet, how you can/should behave toward them and the treatment or response you can expect from them.

115

There are numerous occasions when businessmen and other professionals are expected to make formal aisatsu visits to suppliers, clients and others with whom they have a relationship. These occasions include weddings, deaths, at New Year's, a change of positions, when serious mistakes or accidents occur, and when transferring to new a location.

Aisatsu change with the circumstances. Some call for the presentation of gifts or condolence money; others include congratulations, formal expressions of appreciation, and so on. All require use of various levels of *keigo* (kay-go) or formal Japanese, the right kind of demeanor, the right degree of bowing.

Accomplishing aisatsu properly is an exercise in a broad spectrum of Japanese culture, from the kata-ized way the language is used, the appropriate tone of voice and facial expression, the positioning and moving of the body, to the underlying Confucian philosophy of respect for authority and seniority. Skill in performing aisatsu does not come easily. It requires considerable knowledge, and deliberate practice.

Aisatsu and its role in Japanese behavior should not be ignored or taken lightly by foreigners. It is a vital form of communication and as much of a skill as professional acting.

Denwa no kakekata (Dane-wah no kah-kay-kah-tah)

This is literally "how to use the telephone," which includes not only on what you say but how you say it. In business and other formal situations Japanese are acutely sensitive to language-use because both the level of the language and the way it is used are directly related to the social and professional rank of the individuals involved, and to maintaining proper position and harmony.

Before one can determine which level of language and what tone of voice is appropriate for a given situation, it is necessary to know a lot about the other individual—their age, their company status, their educational level, social status, and so on. If you telephone someone you know, you naturally adopt the "right" kakekata. If you are calling someone with whom you do not already have a well-defined relationship, it is important that you use a relatively high level of language.

Generally speaking, the Japanese will accept non-Japanese telephone etiquette from unknown foreign telephone callers if the callers are polite in a general sense, but they remain especially sensitive to disembodied contacts in which normal physical etiquette is not possible. It is still common for people who have been drilled in Japanese behavior from childhood to bow, sometimes repeatedly, when they are talking to someone on the phone.

Japanese generally will not do business of any kind with anyone whom they have not met face-to-face and established a fairly close relationship. Making the initial contact by phone—to get an. appointment to introduce yourself and begin the process of establishing the necessary relationship—is accepted, but requires considerable skill (especially when the caller is Japanese) in the use of polite forms of the language, in explaining where and how you got the other party's name and why you are calling in the first place.

Salesmen have to be especially skillful in using polite Japanese to avoid upsetting prospects and to get appointments with people they want to see. Listening to one of these polished professionals on the phone is a course in Japanese psychology.

Foreign companies in Japan who use de-Japanized female staff to make their initial telephone contacts with Japanese firms invariably may create a negative image of their firms before they ever get near the Japanese they want to meet. Reason for this is that the foreignized female secretaries or other female staff often either ignore the polite forms of Japanese speech that are part of telephone etiquette or never learned such forms in the first place.

This un-Japanese behavior is repugnant to the etiquette-sensitive Japanese and instantly stamps the foreign company as both insensitive and inexperienced in doing things the Japanese Way. Less tolerant Japanese are likely to label this kind of "foreign" behavior as gross arrogance.

Foreign businessmen doing their own telephoning in Japan are generally treated with some tolerance. How their calls are handled depends on whether or not they speak Japanese well enough to communicate or if they can get someone on the phone who speaks their language. The next factor is whether they have an introduction to a specific individual in the company. If so, they can usually get to that person or at least to a staff member who will take a message.

Foreign callers who do not speak Japanese take a chance that whoever answers the phone speaks enough of their language to communicate with them, or will quickly get someone who can on the phone. Most Japanese companies heavily engaged in international business have telephone operators or receptionists who speak fairly good to good English, but smaller Japanese companies my not.

If the foreign caller has an introduction that is "strong" enough, the individual concerned will probably see .him regardless of what he wants. If the foreign (or Japanese) caller does not have an introduction to a specific person, he may be connected to someone in the General Affairs Department of the company, which handles a variety of miscellaneous activities. It is much wiser—and expected— that callers find out in advance who is in charge of their area of interest.

Denwa no ukekata (Dane-wah no uu-kay-kah-tah)

Not surprisingly, there is also a kata for answering phone calls, but how carefully the established form is followed varies with the standards and training of the individuals and companies concerned. Because callers are not visibly present, this is one area where kata is often ignored by people who are not controlled by their employer or their own standards. The higher the status/rank of the caller, the higher the form of polite Japanese that is expected from the person answering the phone. Until the status of the caller is established it is therefore important that a respectable level of etiquette be used.

One of the set phrases used when answering telephone calls, *Itsumo osewa ni natte imasu* (Ee-sue-moe oh-say-wah nee not-tay ee-mahss), is designed to cover almost any situation. It means "I/we are always being looked after by you," and is more or less an apology in this context. It also has the connotation of "You're always helping me/us" (and we're grateful). This way, no matter who is calling, for whatever purpose, they are made to feel that the call is welcome and that there is some obligation to serve the caller.

Female staff members of larger corporations have to be especially careful about using the proper level of polite Japanese when they answer the phone. Their own male colleagues as well as male callers, particularly those of higher rank, typically judge them as well the company by how they answer the phone.

Hanashi kata (Hah-nah-she kah-tah)

As noted above, *hanashi kata,* or the way one speaks, which includes vocabulary as well as the manner of delivery, plays an important role in Japan's etiquette system, particularly in semi-formal and formal situations when various levels of keigo or "polite language" are expected. On such occasions the minutely prescribed and stylized way of

119

using Japanese has a number of aims: exalting superiors, flattering the other party, avoiding giving offense, maintaining and nurturing harmony, establishing social status—and at times, leaving the listener in the dark.

Ability to use keigo generally marks one as being from a middle or higher class family, and well educated. It is valued as both a social and professional skill and often contributes significantly to one's success. Young female employees of larger Japanese companies are usually given training in hanashi kata in order for them to respond properly to visitors and telephone calls.

Japanese sensitivity to "correct" speech forms, tone of voice, facial expression and overall manner led to the development of precise guidelines for each of these factors. There is a specific hanashi kata for every formal situation that varies with the status of the individuals concerned—their sex, age, rank, relationship to each other and so on.

Some of the relationships that determine proper or accepted hanashi kata are obvious (age differences, sex, etc.). Others are subtle. In order to divine the proper hanashi kata to use, it is necessary to know, or find out as quickly as you can without giving offense in the meantime, what your own status is in relation to the other person. Exchanging name-cards among new business contacts is one of the key ways the Japanese identify each other's status.

The need to determine the appropriate hanashi kata in a new relationship is one of reasons why advance introductions are so important to the Japanese and why they go to such lengths to identify anyone who contacts them without a go-between. Successful use of all the preceding kata is directly related to hanashi kata.

In company and formal settings it is almost always possible to distinguish between inferiors and superiors immediately by the language they use to each other. Relationships and behavior in such settings immediately suggest a very strict military situation involving officers and enlisted men.

How well a Japanese (or foreigner) knows and uses proper hanashi kata is another yardstick for measuring education, cultural accomplishment, social standing, character and worth. Those who are especially skilled in this social art have an advantage and are generally envied and prized.

To achieve a marginally acceptable level of skill in hanashi kata one must master the basic vocabulary and manner of keigo. There are several levels of politeness and subtlety within keigo. The very highest level of keigo is so esoteric that even few Japanese master it. Practically speaking, it is almost another language.

As could be expected, there are also specific kata for preparing and delivering memos *(memo no tori kata* / may-moe no toe-ree kah-tah) and for making reports *(hokoku no shikata* / hoe-koe-kuu no she-kah-tah).

Another very subtle but immensely important kata in the Japanese Way is *tanomi kata* (tah-no-me kah-tah). Tanomi is related to *tanomu* (tah-no-muu), which is defined in dictionary terms as "to ask for, request, beg." As usual, it has far broader and deeper cultural implications than just asking or begging for something.

Tanomi kata incorporates the concept of mutual dependence and mutual benefit in a give-and-take sense, and is closely related to the *nemawashi* (nay-mah-wah-she) system or behind-the-scenes lobbying which the Japanese use in achieving consensus on important matters. The broad purpose of nemawashi is to create an intellectual and emotional environment in which everyone can willingly and energetically support a platform or project, thereby greatly enhancing the prospects of success.

Nemawashi is also sometimes described as planting a seed then unofficially and diplomatically nurturing it by subtle, persuasive techniques to win support for the project. In one form or another, nemawashi is the basis for decision-making in most Japanese companies—although a growing number of internationally oriented companies are in varying stages of adopting top-down decision-making to remain competitive in fast-moving domestic as well as foreign markets.

Tanomi kata, if it is used correctly, can be a powerful tool in making sure that nemawashi works. In simple terms, "tanomi-ing" is asking someone to do something for you or help you achieve some goal when they can hardly refuse because they are in your debt, because you hold the key to their success or failure, because they want to build up obligation that they can collect on later, and so on. It is also common to tanomu someone who is in a position to help you and whom you believe or hope *will* help you because he likes you or because he is a magnanimous soul who will help anyone he feels is sincere and deserves help.

It is common practice for a boss to tanomu his employees when there is a crisis or deadline that has to be met and extraordinary effort is required. On such occasions he will most likely bow and say, *Dozo, yoroshiku . . . tanomimasu,* which more or less means, "I ask you to please do whatever you can!"

Relationships and obligations bound up in the tanomu concept are an intimate part of the amae or indulgent love principle, which is the idealized foundation of Japanese society touched on earlier.

A gung-ho type of personality in a Japanese company may take great delight in being asked to do something special or something especially difficult by a superior because it gives him a chance to show off his spirit and ability. If he fails, however, his reputation will suffer and he will lose status.

When male managers tanomu female employees it is a different matter. It is more like an order phrased in a manner that suggests the women are full permanent members of the group, but in reality takes advantage of the inferior status of the women.

There are also casual uses of tanomu when people use the word to ask family or friends to do something like pick up a gift or remember to put the cat out.

RISK FACTORS IN BUILDING CONSENSUS

One of the reasons for the extraordinary stress in the Japanese way of doing things is the risk factor involved in associating with, communicating with and involving your co-workers in the nemawashi process. If you misread someone's willing to help you or leave out someone who feels he should have been brought into the process, or make any of a number of other miscues, you may suffer setbacks to varying degrees. In serious cases the mistake can be fatal to your career with the company.

A typical example in a medium-sized company: the manager of a department is asked by the senior vice president to do the staff work for a major project. The manager does so, but limits his nemawashi to the vice president and other members of the firm who are directly involved in the project. When the project is completed, it goes to the president for review.

The president becomes very angry at the manager

and kills the project—not because he thought it was poorly done but because he was not quietly (without the vice president knowing about it) brought into the nemawashi process by the manager. He accuses the manager of not knowing how to nemawashi. This leaves the manager with no future in the company and shortly thereafter he resigns.

Because of the risk factor involved in using the nemawashi process it has lost some of its luster among younger managers. They know that if they don't learn to use such tactics, however, their chances of succeeding over the long run in a company are reduced to near zero.

"The difficulty with nemawashi lobbying is that you never know if or when the seeds you are planting are going to sprout," said a manager. "It is a very subtle type of manipulation that depends on appealing to the self-interest of others, with a lot of give-and-take. It is the unseen foundation of business in Japan," he added.

There is also a risk factor involved in ordinary personal relationships within a given group of Japanese. Everyone is always on the lookout for any aberration or deviation from the cultural norm of Japaneseness. You have to be very careful to avoid being trapped by what you say or do. "Most Japanese do not know how to treat others as individuals, and measure everybody by their Japaneseness and the collective interests of the group," said one.

In personal as well as professional dealings within a Japanese company it is always necessary to be aware of hidden meanings and agendas, since people are almost never fully open and candid with each other. Direct communication is seldom complete. Complained one bicultural manager: "Most conversations are just *keshiki* (kay-she-kee)!-formality. You have to decode what the speaker really means."

MANAGING WITHOUT GIVING ORDERS

Aside from new employee orientation and any formal training systems to acquire skills, foreign employees of Japanese companies often complain that no one ever gives them orders or specific instructions about what they are supposed to do, leaving them feeling useless and frustrated. The reason for this is directly linked to kata, to how the Japanese have traditionally been conditioned to teach and learn in business situations.

This silent system of management is based on learning by first observing and listening to general comments and hints, then gradually beginning to do the simplest and most obvious things. In other words, the ancient apprentice system. The third step is to slowly begin to take part in the endless round of discussions that characterize Japanese management, eventually becoming a participating member of the team and thereafter naturally absorbing the knowledge and direction you need.

This traditional type of "instruction" is literally known as *mi-narai* (me-nah-rye) or "learn by watching." While still common, it is coming under increasing criticism by younger people who say it wastes time, reinforces outdated methods of teaching needed skills, and emphasizes role behavior. Managing without giving direct orders is called *meirei no shikata* (may-e-ray no she-kah-tah), or "way of giving orders." It does not consist of giving orders in the Western sense. It is creating a situation in which individual workers know what they are supposed to do, are given the necessary incentive to do it, and are rewarded when they do. The system is designed to avoid singling individuals out, to diffuse responsibility and to give each person the opportunity to do his or her best—always within the confines of the group and its interests.

What might be called a sub-division of meirei no kata is *shiji no dashi kata* (she-jee no dah-shee kah-tah) or "way of giving direction," which follows the same guidelines and has the same goals. There is also an extension of the meirei no shikata concept that covers how employees are expected to react to it: *meirei no ukekata,* or "how to receive/ accept meirei." The essence of meirei no ukekata is that employees are expected to carry out the wishes of management in a way that will please everyone and enhance the image/status of the group. This includes the idea that employees will use their own initiative, motivate themselves and not let management or the group down.

In keeping with the group-oriented shame factor as a control mechanism in Japanese society, the most devastating way to get better performance by individuals is to point out the need for improvement in front of their colleagues. The power of this approach obviously lies in the fact that because the individual's failings, which effect the whole group, are made public, he has no other place to go, and becomes subject to pressure from his own co-workers.

THE JAPANESE WAY OF WORKING

Most larger Japanese companies are microcosms of the kata system at work, with *shigoto no shikata* (she-go-toe no she-kah-tah) or "the way of working" playing a central role. Shigoto no shikata sounds simple enough, but it goes far beyond the obvious surface facets of technical ability and physical or mental performance. It encompasses the whole Japanese work ethic, from groupism and harmony to the built-in compulsion for continuous improvement in the process.

Virtually every aspect of work in a Japanese company begins and ends with whatever group one belongs to. The groups are structured hierarchically as pyramids. Relationships within the groups are based on longevity and rank within the group, with these two factors often being synonymous in the case of male employees.

In most cases, the lowest ranking members of any group are female, and these are usually the newest and youngest members of the group. Except in still rare cases, women in larger Japanese companies do not rise to become leaders of groups, sections or departments.

The first priority in a group is the harmony, integrity and survival of the group. The second priority is to achieve the goals set for the group, and, if humanly possible, to over-achieve them because the kata-ized system conditions people to regard anything less than maximum effort and maximum results as a shameful failure.

The shigoto no shikata concept includes the state of mind of all the members of the group concerned, their attitudes about the company, their group and their work responsibilities, as well as how they behave in their

127

personal relations within the group and toward outsiders. The concept covers what they say and how they say it. It requires them to take pride in their group and company, to go about their work in a •warm, sincere, trusting and positive manner and to be gracious and hospitable to clients and other visitors. The aim of shigoto no shikata is to create an environment in which the contribution of each member transcends the goal of just getting the work done.

Shigoto no shikata is permeated by two other concepts that are constantly on the lips of the Japanese: *gambaru* (gahm-bah-rue) and *issho-kenmeiyaru* (ee-show-ken-may-ee yah-rue). Gambaru means to persevere; to never give up. Isshokenmei yaru means to do one's best. When these concepts are energetically combined it results in a high quality of effort and greatly enhances achievement.

Each person in a Japanese group is constantly monitored and evaluated by higher-ups on a subconscious as well as conscious level. The individual's mood along with every comment and action, on both a personal and business basis, automatically "registers" on the shigoto no shikata scale of measuring people.

If the individual doesn't measure up in terms of putting the group first, maintaining harmony and demonstrating a "fighting spirit" on behalf of the group and the company— no matter how hard he may actually work—he will invariably receive low marks that will eventually result in him being side-tracked off of the promotion escalator and out of the mainstream of management.

In such a system it is virtually impossible for anyone to enter a group except at the bottom or at the top, and those who enter at the top are almost never fully accepted by those below them. If the newcomers are not extremely careful in dealing with the group, submerging most of their own personalities and individualistic tendencies, the group will reject them the same way the human body rejects the invasion of incompatible matter.

When the "foreign matter" introduced into a Japanese company group is indeed a foreigner, he or she is generally kept outside of the inner circle of the group, either as an accessory or as a temporary tool. If an effort is made to actually integrate the foreigner into the group, the situation becomes highly charged with all kinds of possibilities—most of which spell trouble for all concerned.

In most cases the foreigner concerned is not capable of blending into the group because he cannot speak Japanese at all or not well enough to eliminate all verbal communication barriers. Most foreign employees of Japanese companies are even less capable of communicating properly in non-verbal cultural terms. Their physical appearance alone is enough to set them apart as different, as not a homogenized, trustworthy, dependable segment of the same cultural cloth.

This means that the foreigner is a side-car with a square wheel. How long he stays in the group and how efficiently he functions is based on his ability to persevere in the face of unending visible and invisible barriers, how tolerant the Japanese members decide to be on his behalf, and if he is making a significant contribution to the goals of the group and these contributions are such that no Japanese can easily replace him.

On a personal basis many Japanese are characteristically tolerant of the non-Japanese behavior of foreigners. In a work or professional group context, however, especially if there is even a hint of direct competition, the Japanese are more apt to take a highly intolerant stance and resist passively or aggressively, depending on the situation.

In Japanese companies a primary criterion used by personnel officers when considering new employees (to bring in at the bottom) is whether or not they think the candidates can be psychologically molded to fit their shigoto no shikata. The huge, multi-faceted Tokyu Corporation (railroads, hotels, resorts, restaurants, etc.) traditionally went well beyond carefully screening new employees. After they were hired, all employees-male, female, married as well as unmarried—were required to live in a dormitory for one year and work at menial jobs in one of the corporation's many divisions. They had to turn in weekly reports on their experiences and what they learned. One of the goals of this program was to weld the employees into a cohesive group with the proper Tokyu spirit.

Fierce groupism in Japanese companies is one of the primary reasons why the headhunting industry took so long to develop in Japan (there are now over two hundred and fifty recruiting firms, but the turnover is still relatively small), and why hostile takeovers of companies are rare. Even friendly takeovers in Japan must contend with the groupism factor, sometimes until the original managers in the companies retire or die. Twenty years after the merger of the Daiichi and Kangyo banks, the presidency of Daiichi-Kangyo Bank continued to be alternated between surviving officers of the two former banks.

Japanese compulsion for corporate and national conformity is so strong that it covers not only attitude and behavior, but physical appearance as well. The pre-1945 stories of how Japanese with anything other than straight, black hair and purely Oriental facial features were subject to severe discrimination would seem to be ancient history. However, these feelings, on a lesser but still significant scale, remain alive today for most Japanese.

Many older Japanese teachers take it upon themselves to continue this cultural bias in favor of absolute conformity, forcing their students to look and behave as much alike as possible. Most of the "new breed" of young Japanese one sees in the entertainment districts on weekends and holidays, with their outlandish clothing and hairdos, return to the traditional mold of sameness when they go to work on Monday mornings.

In theory, the conformity that is demanded within a Japanese group makes total equality an absolute. Everyone is not only supposed to think and act alike, they are also supposed to be equal in ability. Those who are more able than others are expected to behave as if they were no more talented than the next person. Any sign of superior ability is likely to provoke instant envy, resistance and, if the able person flaunts his ability, extreme hatred.

Examples of how this syndrome works, and how subtle it can be, are commonplace. The recommendation of an individual for a special assignment in a Japanese company can set off a series of stressful, unhappy events. Instead of being grateful that his ability and loyalty have been recognized, the person is more likely to fear that being singled out from his colleagues may result in them turning against him. Or he may become suspicious that he is being set up by someone who wants to eventually get rid of him.

In any event it is absolutely essential that he approach the assignment with the utmost humility and painstakingly seek the understanding and approval of his co-workers.

It has been characteristic throughout much of Japan's history that the man of extraordinary talent and ambition did not rise to a position of leadership because the group equality-above-all-else syndrome resulted in his being ignored or ostracized. In fact, the tendency has been and still is, to a significant degree, for the mediocre man to be chosen as leader because he will not create envy or upset the wa of the group. This is especially true in political and educational circles and within professional associations.

Historical exceptions to this pattern were common during periods of social upheaval and war, and are now becoming more common in business circles as the system evolves, particularly in companies that have globalized their operations and must now compete on an international basis.

Japan's kata-ized conformity factor is naturally responsible for the follow-the-leader syndrome that still prevails throughout all levels of social and economic life. Examples of fads sweeping the country are legend.

Japanese as well as foreign marketers take regular advantage of the overwhelming desire of most Japanese to "keep up with the Suzuki's" in dress, household appliances, recreational equipment or whatever. Sales people know instinctively that if they can sell a product to a leading company, other companies will generally follow suit whether or not they need the item.

One foreign ice-cream company used the follow-the-leader syndrome in the Japanese makeup to introduce its product into the market in a simple but very astute way. When the company opened its first shop, in winter, it hired a large number of people every day tor several days to form a line extending from the counter in the shop to well down the block. Seeing the long line, other people joined it in droves, making the new ice-cream an extraordinary success in a short period of time.

DANGERS OF SPEAKING ENGLISH

Every foreign firm, joint venture and foreign-affiliated firm in Japan has its share of *Eigo-ya* (Aa-ee-go-yah), which is a rather derogatory term for "English speakers." These people have traditionally been resented by other Japanese staff members who do not speak English. Still today, most non-English speakers resent the familiarity that develops between the Eigo-ya and the foreign staff. They resent the role played by the English speakers as interpreters and liaison between the foreigners and Japanese management. They perceive the Eigo-ya as being favored and privileged— and often they are.

Japan's Eigo-ya are fully aware of the sensitivity of their position, and react to their situation in a variety of ways. Some of those who feel that the foreign side cannot do without them sometimes choose to take advantage of their power to lord it over their Japanese co-workers. Others go to extremes to maintain harmonious relations with their Japanese colleagues.

Eigo-ya who do try to maintain wa with their Japanese

colleagues are often forced into being two-faced. Others choose to be two-faced. When they are talking to and interacting with the foreign side they pretend to agree with them and support them. When they go back to the Japanese side, they criticize and laugh at the foreigners. Eigo-ya in this category often contrive to thwart the efforts of the foreign staff to prevent them from succeeding and eventually get them replaced by Japanese.

Employees of especially conservative Japanese companies who speak English with any degree of fluency often feel compelled to downplay their ability or conceal it entirely to avoid negative reactions of envy and resentment from their co-workers which can adversely affect their careers.

The position of Westernized or internationalized Japanese executives in Japan is also often precarious to a degree that suggests paranoia among their still one hundred percent *Japanese* Japanese co-workers. In foreign and foreign-affiliated companies in Japan the scenario almost invariably follows a familiar pattern. The foreign side brings in a Western-educated Japanese executive, usually in a sales or marketing position. He immediately begins doing exactly what he was hired for—attempting to initiate an aggressive, positive approach to sales.

His problems with the Japanese staff also begin immediately. In addition to being resented for his Western education and intimate-appearing relationship with the foreign bosses, his independent-minded aggressiveness clashes head-on with the Japanese system of groupism and consensus-building. When he tries to short-circuit the subtle time-consuming nemawashi shikata, or way of consensus building, he often seals his fate.

134

More aggressive members of the Japanese staff characteristically begin a covert campaign to oust him by not following through on his programs and otherwise sabotaging everything he tries to do. When it becomes obvious to the foreign managers that nothing is going to be accomplished as long as the Westernized Japanese remains in place—and they often blame him—they move him to a less sensitive position, transfer him to a branch or somewhere else, or fire him.

COPING WITH A HUMBLE MODE

Japanese often appear as passive, naive, helpless and even simple-minded, to uninitiated Westerners. This appearance seems to trigger an uncontrollable compulsion in many Westerners to "help" the humble, polite, grateful-acting Japanese. In actuality, such behavior has traditionally been a cultural cloak that the Japanese wore to *avoid* appearing aggressive, capable, independent-minded and individualistic—all of which were taboo in the Japanese context of things.

This facet of Japanese behavior remains characteristic of the majority, but there is a growing movement among bureaucrats, businessmen and diplomats to learn how to communicate and negotiate aggressively in the Western manner. This movement "officially" began in the 1960s with the introduction of Dale Carnegie courses by the Japan Institute of Human Relations (JIHRX which now graduates several thousand student-businessmen each year.

Efforts of the Japanese to wean themselves away from their traditional humble mode received an extraordinary boost in the early 1980s with the success of the Japanese language edition of Lee Iacocca's auto-biography. In the book Iacocca credited a Dale Carnegie course with having contributed significantly to his own success, causing a rush among Japanese to enroll in the Carnegie courses.

The still typically passive manner of most Japanese is not necessarily a contrived act deliberately designed to mislead Westerners. It is the way the Japanese are forced to behave to conform to their own social mores. At the same time, however, the Japanese are smart enough to have recognized long ago that their apparent polite passivity gives them a considerable edge when they are dealing with aggressive, forthright Westerners who are not familiar with their type of role playing.

Americans in particular seem to have an acute compulsion to fill every silence, every vacuum—to talk, talk, talk and tell all. The Japanese, on the other hand, typically soak up everything that is loose and give nothing in return. A significant degree of Japan's success can be traced to this one cultural characteristic, which one Japanese commentator describes as a "black hole" syndrome. Often all the Japanese have to do when they want something from foreigners is bow, smile, sit back and wait.

Kata-ized conditioning in the Japanese way makes it difficult to impossible for Japanese businessmen to react immediately or quickly to new proposals and unexpected events. They have been trained to react in exactly the opposite manner—to say little or nothing upon first hearing a proposition; to take days, weeks or months to think about it and discuss it before coming to a consensus.

Foreign businessmen who are not familiar with this

136

cultural pattern often react in the wrong way. A common scenario is for the foreign side to be filled with euphoria and excitement at how well they made their own presentation and how "great" the deal is, then be on the edge of their seats with expectation. When the Japanese do not respond quickly, the foreign side is first puzzled, then disappointed. Some Westerners become quite angry, blaming the Japanese for "leading them on."

In so many instances the foreign side reveals all of its experience, insights and technology up front and is left with no bargaining power and a strong feeling of frustration.

The most effective way to deal with Japanese businessmen without giving the store away in advance is to emphasize that you (or your company) can help them succeed and look good at the same time, and stop there, resisting your own impulse to bare all, and all efforts by the intensely inquisitive Japanese to ferret out every last piece of information. Once you reveal the precise details of *how* you can benefit a Japanese company your position is greatly weakened because it is their nature to absorb the message and reject the messenger.

Another aspect of this characteristic behavior is that the concept of technology and experience having proprietary value was traditionally alien to the Japanese and is still only partially developed. New-found friends with connections or special knowledge are subject to being used endlessly—with an occasional small gift or meal regarded as sufficient remuneration.

Once a foreign company signs a contract with a Japanese firm the tendency is for the Japanese side to presume that it can obtain any service, any information the foreign company possesses regardless of the limited nature of the contract. Summarily refusing to comply with such requests can seriously damage a relationship. It is necessary to very formally and diplomatically explain that such requests cost time and money and cannot be honored without a new understanding that details the additional fees to be paid.

ETIQUETTE AS A WEAPON

Foreign businessmen visiting Japan on brief trips typically get a false impression of what they think they have accomplished. The full force of the courtesy kata of the Japanese system is always in play on first meetings. The visitor, especially if he represents a large well-known company, usually gets royal treatment. Representatives of lesser firms as well are normally treated with a degree and quality of hospitality that is very seductive.

Personal attention, hospitality and entertainment showered on foreign visitors by the Japanese is invariably enough to soften them up. When this is combined with the Japanese custom of avoiding direct criticism, confrontation and clear-cut rejections, it becomes a formidable barrier to understanding. Not being familiar with the Japanese way and therefore unable to recognize Japanese reality, many visitors mislead themselves into believing that everything is going great, that they are making progress.

Foreign businessmen taking up residence in Japan have important advantages over visitors on brief trips, but they too face similar problems until they learn how the drama of business is played by the Japanese. Even after the newcomers learn the system and get their own act down pat, however, they generally find that their efficiency drops off dramatically. It simply takes considerably longer to do things because of the Japanese Way.

Among other things, the typical foreign businessman in Japan cannot make his own phone calls unless he is calling someone who speaks English or some other foreign language. Except in rare cases where very high-paid bilingual secretarial help is available, he cannot dictate a letter or fax. Secretaries who can take shorthand are rarer still.

Foreign visitors often require guides and interpreters to help them find the Japanese companies they want to visit, and even with help this can be a time-consuming ordeal because most streets in Japanese cities do not have names. Even more confusing, addresses of buildings have absolutely nothing to do with whatever street they are on. Furthermore, many buildings do not have their addresses posted anywhere. You can be in front of and sometimes actually inside of a building and not be able to confirm that it is the building you want if you don't read or speak Japanese.

What the foreign businessman can often accomplish in his home country with one or two phone calls more often than not takes several face-to-face meetings over a period of weeks or months to accomplish in Japan. Usually it takes from three to five or more meetings with Japanese businessmen, usually one to three weeks apart, before any kind of results are achieved—even if it is just to pursue the dialogue.

During this drawn-out getting acquainted process, the foreign businessman is expected to adhere closely to the kata-ized behavior patterns expected by the Japanese, including—and especially—good-humored patience, responding energetically and thoroughly to what often seems to be an unending series of questions and requests for additional information, ceremonial politeness, sincerity, dependability, and so on. See *Businessman's Quick Guide to Japan* (Charles E. Tuttle/Yen Books) and *Japanese Etiquette & Ethics in Business* (NTC Business Books).

Cultural gaps between Western and Japanese business ways that are encountered by bilingual and bicultural foreign consultants in Japan are especially revealing.

Said one: "When I was first retained by a major Japanese company the people I was involved with treated me as an outsider because of my foreign face. But once they got to know me and recognized that I could communicate with them and wanted to help them solve their problems, they ostensibly accepted me as a member of their group, supported me in my research and encouraged me to recommend new approaches. I was treated as a *men/o Nihonjin* (may-ee-yoe Nee-hone-jee) or 'honorary Japanese.'

"When I made my recommendations, however, they could not accept them and immediately reverted to treating me as an outsider. My status as an honorary Japanese lasted only as long as I did not represent a threat to their way of doing things."

This consultant said his thirty-five years in Japan had taught him that it is impossible for the Japanese to develop the kind of relationships with non-Japanese that they have with each other. "Total language and cultural fluency has nothing to do with it," he said. "Their cultural programming is simply too strong for them to overcome. Distrust of foreigners is too deeply engrained in them."

At the same time, loyalty in Japan is a kata, not a

universal principle. The Japanese are conditioned to be loyal to groups and to expect the same degree of loyalty in return. If a group fails to demonstrate the degree of loyalty they expect, they readily shift their allegiance.

Japan's real or perceived lack of principles in conducting their business and political affairs is at the bottom of much of the distrust of Japan that exists around the world. Says one foreign executive in Tokyo: "While the Japanese may earn the respect of others for their accomplishments, it will be a long time before they are truly admired, trusted and emulated by those who know them well."

The cultural exclusivity of the Japanese has another aspect that is the source of many of the problems and friction between them and non-Japanese. They unconsciously distinguish between communicating in the Japanese language and in foreign languages. Communication in English or other foreign languages is often not regarded as "official" or binding, as representing the real world.

This factor impacts on virtually all relations the Japanese have with non-Japanese. Most foreign businessmen attempting to deal with their Japanese counterparts are first handicapped because they cannot speak Japanese. They then bring in interpreters, who are usually Japanese, presuming this solves the communication problem, only to discover later that the Japanese understanding of the situation between the two parties is quite different. "What transpires in a foreign language is in another dimension," said a veteran consultant.

Another critical aspect of this common situation is that the English-speaking Japanese interpreter brought into the scenario is almost never the perfect conduit. He may understand and sympathize with the foreign side when speaking to them in English but he must also understand and sympathize with the Japanese side when speaking to them in Japanese. If he translates exactly what the foreign side says, in every cultural sense, he will likely offend or confuse the Japanese side. If he tries to convey the exact cultural flavor and meaning of the Japanese dialogue, it will invariably mislead the foreign side.

AVOIDING EMOTIONAL BLOCKS

Japanese emotionalism, usually masked behind smiles and their stylized etiquette, can be a serious obstacle to establishing personal or business relationships with foreigners. If the outsider gets off on the wrong foot by being just a little too pushy, by being impolite (by Japanese standards) in action or in tone of voice, it sets up an emotional block in the minds of the Japanese.

In addition, Japanese take business very seriously and follow traditional etiquette in their office behavior. There is a minimum of joking and banter among office staff. Horseplay is virtually unthinkable. It is very difficult for Japanese to take an undisciplined, informal foreign businessman seriously.

Many foreign businessmen, habitually use curse words and other forms of vulgar speech in their daily business conversations. Unless you know a Japanese intimately and know for certain that he accepts such behavior from you, this kind of speech is dangerous because it will almost always prejudice the Japanese against you.

Once an emotional barrier has been erected, for whatever reason, it is almost certain that the Japanese will not get involved with you even though they may continue a meeting or presentation for hours, and even agree to other meetings.

The right kata to take is the quiet, "modest interest" and "exemplary" behavior mode, while working to create confidence in you and your company. There is really no viable way to speed up this process when you are in the position of seller or petitioner. If you have something the Japanese want and they are courting you, they will probably already have gone through their preliminary investigations and consensus-building routine, and may appear to be acting very swiftly.

As mentioned earlier, business relations in Japan are primarily personal relations, with a significant "give and take" element, especially in the sense of performing favors and repaying obligations. Individuals deliberately do favors for others, which includes wining and dining them, giving them gifts and treating them to golf, etc., expecting that they will eventually be repaid in new business, more business or just continued business.

The Japanese press frequently reports on exceptional cases in which a government office or company spends hundreds of millions of yen in "entertainment" in an attempt to influence business decisions—something that is not exactly unique to Japan, but which is practiced there as a sanctified custom.

Japanese are, of course, fully aware of what is going on when someone gives them gifts and treats them to more than casual hospitality, and they often make a point of returning the favors in kind in order to avoid incurring business obligations they don't want to, or can't, fulfill. This striving for a balance between favors and obligations is a delicate kata-ized factor in the Japanese business system.

Reciprocating favors is not always a balancing of accounts, however. It is also used as a sign that a business

143

relationship is going to occur or is going well—a situation that is usually very obvious from the tone and mood of the individuals involved.

THE KATA OF RANK

In Japan's vertically structured hierarchical society rank has traditionally been a key factor in the kata-ization process, beginning with showing respect to parents, elders and superiors in behavior as well as language, distinguishing between the sexes, and following the precise etiquette expected in the various situations encountered on a regular basis.

To behave properly toward individual Japanese in the Japanese cultural environment, it is essential to know their rank in relation to your own. During Japan's feudal age, social class could usually be discerned from wearing apparel and whether or not one was armed with two swords—one short and one long (the short sword was for use in close fighting and to commit suicide when this ritual was required).

Wearing apparel was just as kata-ized as behavior, and was prescribed by the shogunate government. Different categories of tradespeople wore similar outfits that clearly identified their profession and their social class. Only the ruling samurai class were permitted to wear certain types of robes, along with swords.

As with many other facets of Japan's kata-ized culture, the codifying of rank began in the Imperial Court. Prince Shotoku, who ruled as regent in the 7th century, was responsible for adopting the "Twelve Cap" Chinese system for grading and ranking members of the court and nobles. Each of the twelve different ranks was designated by the color and style of the headgear.

Clearly visible symbols of class or rank are no longer common in Japan, but rank, whether in the business world, politics or the professions, is still a vital factor in relationships. The Japanese remain very sensitive to class and rank, and behave accordingly.

As a general rule Japanese do not expect foreigners to know and follow all aspects of Japanese etiquette, especially those having to do with rank. But the foreigner who does not know something about this factor in Japanese life and make use of it is handicapped in a variety of ways. Among other things, ignorance of proper Japanese rank etiquette indelibly stamps the foreigner as an outsider—and substantiates the constant Japanese claim that foreigners have difficulty in Japan because they do not know and follow the system.

SITTING IN THE RIGHT PLACE

No foreign businessman has been to Japan without experiencing the shikata of seating. In keeping with their superior-inferior hierarchical ranking system, the Japanese are extremely sensitive to where people sit and automatically seat everyone according to their rank or status at the moment.

Formal seating kata in Japan also go back to the days of Prince Shotoku in the 7th century when he adopted the "Twelve Cap" Chinese system of designating ranks among courtiers. The prince incorporated the Chinese court custom of seating people in a descending order from the immediate vicinity of the emperor outward and on successively lower levels. This custom, adapted to fit the circumstances, eventually permeated Japanese society.

In the Japanese context, as in other cultures, every

room or space has a "head" or "power place" where the ranking individual normally sits or stands. Ranking guests are also commonly accorded this honor. The "power seat" is called *kanri za* (kah-me zah) or "upper seat" in Japanese. In a private Japanese style home or a Japanese style room in an inn or restaurant the kami za (on the reed-mat floor) is the space nearest the *tokonoma* (toe-koe-no-mah), a "beauty alcove" used for the display of flower arrangements, scrolls or other works of art.

In a Western style room, business office, conference room or hall, the head of the room where ranking people are seated is usually the farthest from the door and/or nearest the main window side. In a car, the kami za is the back seat behind the driver. In an elevator it is the center of the elevator in the back, away from the door.

Japanese are constantly guiding foreigners to the seat considered proper for their rank and status, sometimes physically propelling them when they show reluctance to go to the "head" table or the "power seat"— and when they demonstrate ignorance of the custom. Foreign businessmen dealing with Japanese should be equally sensitive to this seating shikata and follow it when they have Japanese guests.

Another important shikata in treating business visitors is to accompany them to the elevator if on an upper floor and to the door if on the first floor. Japanese hosts also push the elevator button as an additional courtesy.

CALLING PEOPLE NAMES

In keeping with the tiered ranking of individuals within Japanese society, titles became an integral part of the kata-ized culture. In private as well as public life, it eventually

146

became more common to use titles than personal names. Titles were based on official and professional rank and on occupation. When based on occupation, the titles often identified the trade—*Daiku San* (dike-sahn) was Mr. Carpenter, *Omawari San* (Oh-mah-wah-ree Sahn) was Mr. Policeman, and so on.

Titles are another facet of traditional Japanese culture that have stood the test of time and the new waves of "internationalization" that began washing over the islands in 1945. The importance and use of titles is especially conspicuous in business where, on managerial levels, they are routinely used instead of names. Instead of a section manager being Mr. Kato, he is usually addressed as *Ka Cho* (Kah Choe) or "Section Manager," and so on up the middle-management and executive ladder to the chairman of the board—who is referred to as *Kai Cho* (Kie Choe).

Commented a young foreign businessman in Tokyo: "I learned the hard way that one calls a president of a company 'President Sato, not 'Mr. Sato.'"

EXCHANGING NAME-CARDS

Following the official end of Japan's feudal system in 1868, name-cards soon replaced apparel and other visible signs of rank. Because of the importance of rank, name-cards have continued to play a vital role in the country's formalized business world. It is often said, with a substantial amount of truth, that in Japan if you do not have a name-card, you don't exist.

Of course, the exchanging of name-cards—*meishi kokan* (may-she koe-kahn)—is a stylized process. In the first place, it is "correct" for name-cards to be kept in a card case to prevent them from becoming soiled or worn.

When introduced by someone else, the Japanese customarily face each other, exchange cards (purists hold their cards with both hands when proffering them), and say "My name is So & So" (even though the go-between has already announced the names), while handing their cards over. They then glance quickly at the other person's company, title and name, and bow according to the degree of respect and honor the other person is entitled to while saying "I'm pleased to meet you," or one of the other stock introductory greetings. You do *not* give your title when introducing yourself.

Once this ritual is over it is customary for each person to again look at the other party's name-card, this time studying it more carefully to make sure of the individual's name, company and title. If the individuals then sit down at a coffee table or conference table the practice is to lay the other person's card on the table in front of you so you can glance at it during the conversation to remind yourself of the other person's name and title.

From this point on, how the Japanese react to the new acquaintance, the language they use and their physical behavior, is determined to a considerable degree by the rank of the other person's company in the hierarchy of the business world, the person's rank within the company and the relations between the two companies.

The meishi kokan ceremony is simple in form but it is important to do it right—to follow the right kata—if you want to impress the Japanese and develop a smooth, unstressed relationship with them. Name-card exchanges at first meetings tell the recipients a great deal about each other, especially if both of the parties are Japanese since they can usually make an instant judgment about the relative rank and importance of the new acquaintance, based on the size of the other person's company and their position.

STRUCTURE OF A JAPANESE OFFICE

Some post-1945 Japanese companies that are primarily involved in business with the international community have adapted varying degrees of Western style office arrangements. However, most companies adhere fully or in part to the traditional system which is based on a specific form designed to identify the rank of the staff, to facilitate communication (which is invariably verbal), and to maximize group-oriented efficiency.

Office structure is based on *bu* (boo) or department and *ka* (kah) or sections within the department. The standard desk arrangement is very similar to a classroom made up of several "grades" or sections. The department manager is at the head of the room, facing several rows of desks that are generally positioned back-to-back (so the occupants face each other), with a head desk at the top of the formation, facing the other desks.

Section managers sit at the head desk of the oblong-shaped formation, with a view of all of their staff. Their assistants normally sit at: the first desk to their right. The rest of the line-up usually indicates the seniority of the individual members. The more senior the staff members, the closer they are to the manager. Newcomers generally start out at or near the bottom of the line-up.

This open-bay type of arrangement is typically Japanese in that the formation contributes to both the concept and the function of a team. Everybody can see what others are doing and can hear all conversations that take place within some distance from their desks. Foreigners who have worked in these section formations say that all the members have their antenna up at all times and that news of any kind sweeps over the whole office in waves.

Each section functions as a highly trained unit, very much like a football squad, with the exception that the section leader does not call out moves play-by-play. Projects are minutely discussed in advance and the process of implementing them is also carefully worked out beforehand, with each member on the team knowing his or her role. The manager is there to answer questions and make suggestions, but not to run a one-man show.

Section managers hold frequent consultations with their staffs, with one another and with department managers. Department managers are coaches who seldom go onto the playing field and may give only a few pep talks a year to the whole group.

Managers in most Japanese companies work their way up from the bottom, spending time in several different sections and departments, cementing relationships with their co-workers and gaining an overall view of the company's activities. Depending on the company, it takes from seven to nine years for a managerial candidate to rise to the rank of assistant section chief, sixteen years to become the head of a section, and twenty-two to twenty-six years to become a department manager.

Except for the command function, Japanese company groups are similar to most military units, which, of course, are examples of kata-ization that are well known worldwide. Japanese company sections are the equivalent of military squads, which usually have eight to twelve members. Departments are the equivalent of companies made up of several squads.

In the Japanese system a great many project proposals begin •with section chiefs (squad leaders who are the equivalent of corporals or sergeants in smaller and medium-sized firms and lieutenants in larger companies) and work their way up through the chain to the executive level. Since the section chiefs are in the trenches and are expected to know more about what is going on than higher management, particularly when their project concerns a process, their proposals are often approved in part or in w^{h}ole.

DEALING WITH THE CONSENSUS KATA

It is particularly important for the foreign businessman dealing with Japan to be totally familiar with the kata of decision-making in matters relating to external activities. It is typically a quasi-democratic process that involves anywhere from a few to dozens of people discussing a subject down to the bone and then coming to a consensus about what to do or not to do—this despite the growing influence of Western style decision-making in some Japanese companies.

Unlike typical Western executives who can make a variety of decisions on their own, the authority of most individual Japanese managers, including top executives, is still very limited. Most exceptions to this rule are found in companies where the founder is still serving as the chief executive officer, and in the overseas branches and subsidiaries of major corporations where decisions must be tailored to the local scene.

Because the still prevailing Japanese system of decision-making on new projects involves many people, it generally cannot be done quickly. Attempts to speed up the process by pressure from the outside may succeed temporarily but almost always back-fire in the long run because the pressure is resented and the decision may not be to the liking of people who are able to sabotage it. Some critics of the Japanese system of decision-making say that Japanese decision makers, collectively speaking, are drilled in people analysis, not problem analysis, since their success depends more on their abilities to persuade or manipulate their colleagues than on defining problems and opportunities. This is no doubt true to a degree, but certainly not to the point that it prevents the Japanese from being very successful at solving problems.

The larger the Japanese company the more "bottoms up" proposals presented by different departments. At any one time dozens of different proposals may be in competition with each other, which is another reason why it takes a relatively long time for a proposal to be approved or disapproved in a large Japanese company.

In some cases there are several competing proposals for the same project. Often the best parts of all of the plans end up in one plan—a very effective method of improving the overall quality of planning but another time-consuming process that often frustrates outsiders.

"Foreign businessmen must not only learn how to nemawashi to succeed in Japan, they should also be aware that the process is frequently abused by many Japanese," warns an American businessman-writer who resides in Tokyo. He explains: "It is common for a person with whom you are doing business or trying to do business to make an appointment with you and ask if he can bring along someone else from his company. It often turns out that the only purpose of the second individual is to pick your brain. When you get such calls it is advisable to find out exactly who the other person is and why they want to meet you."

Brain-picking in Japan, as mentioned earlier, goes well beyond the nemawashi process. There appears to be a natural inclination in the Japanese to learn everything they can about everything—a trait that has contributed enormously to their extraordinary economic success. Japanese businessmen and others ask questions and listen with an intensity, and to such lengths, that it often drives their foreign counterparts to distraction. When this cultural habit is combined with the tendency of Westerners, especially Americans, to automatically assume a teaching or lecturing manner in the presence of Japanese (and others), it gives the Japanese a double advantage.

Many Japanese companies still use the traditional *ringi sho* (reen-ghee show) system of writing out proposals and circulating them to all the people concerned, first on the middle management level and then going up the ladder to top executives. If the document survives the scrutiny of middle and upper level managers, the CEO usually goes along with it. When the ringi sho is used, nemawashi still takes place, with the document as the focus of the discussions. Authorized readers sign it if they are in agreement, thus diluting responsibility for any adverse consequences.

Younger members of Japanese companies are chaffing under the nemawashi system of decision-making. Some are aggressively pushing for changes that would allow them to participate more directly in decisions and to get individual recognition for their successful efforts. There is a lot of talk about such changes and how far they have already gone, but a significant portion of this impression is exaggerated, especially where major companies are concerned. Fast decisions made by individual managers in large firms are still rare.

FOLLOWING THE CHAIN OF COMMAND

In addition to the kata of appropriate manners and language, business and professional relationships in Japan have a strict protocol that is very similar to a rigid military code. One of the most important facets of this code is paying special attention to the chain of command and being careful not to get anyone's nose out of joint by going over his head.

Just like a strictly run military outfit, the Japanese have been conditioned to expect everyone, insiders as well as outsiders, to follow the prescribed command chain in all relationships.

For example, if a New York businessman who knows the president of a Japanese company goes to Japan and visits the president without going through the firm's New York branch office it is a breach of protocol that can be serious. The branch manager of the Japanese company will feel slighted and left out and will likely bear a grudge against the New York businessman from then on.

Depending on the circumstances, the Japanese branch manager in New York may become suspicious of the motives of the foreign businessman and thereafter mistrust him. Proper protocol, even if you have known the president in Japan for years and don't know the branch manager at all, is to play it by the kata-ized rules of order. The Japanese are innately suspicious of anybody who does not conform to established patterns of behavior.

While all Japanese behavior is obviously not controlled or directed by kata as pervasive as those governing the practice of karate-do, Western businessmen should keep in mind that there is, however, a kata for every aspect of Japanese mentality and behavior, and that failure to recognize and take the appropriate kata into consideration creates discomfort and, if too pronounced, can doom any endeavor.

Another typical example: a group of Japanese businessmen come to New York to look into investment opportunities in the U.S. The New York branch of their bank in Japan provides them with a staff member to act as their interpreter at a meeting with a group of American businessmen.

Despite having been carefully briefed by a veteran *Japanese* consultant to keep their presentation general and give only an overview (with the details to be provided later in written form), the American side makes a profusely detailed, highly technical presentation that totally floors the interpreter and leaves the visiting Japanese delegation squirming in their seats with anger, embarrassment and boredom.

The American side becomes increasingly aware that the interpreter is doing a very bad job and they become upset and angry that the bilingual Japanese consultant retained by their company doesn't jump in and take over the role of interpreter. The meeting is an unpleasant experience for everyone.

The Japanese consultant later explained to his American colleagues that the kata applying to the way the Japanese conduct interpersonal relations prevented him from stepping in and taking over. Everyone on the Japanese side would have been shamed. The Japanese employee would have lost face and standing with his bank's clients as well as with the American side in a way that would never be forgotten—or forgiven.

The visiting Japanese businessmen would have understood the presentation if the Japanese consultant had stepped in, but they too are bound by the dictates of kata designed to maintain face and harmony, and the negative factors involved in the situation would have outweighed the benefits.

"It was an extremely painful situation for me," said the Japanese consultant. "I, more than anyone, could see that the meeting was going very badly, but I couldn't stop my American colleagues and say, 'Hey! You're making a big mistake! You're doing exactly the opposite of what I advised you to do!' And as a Japanese I couldn't insult the Japanese group by behaving in a manner that would destroy my ability to work with them in the future."

Of course, this kind of cross-cultural encounter appears silly and counter-productive to the logical-minded, rational thinking Westerner. The point is that the kata of Japan often negate logic, and that kata often cannot be ignored, regardless of how "dumb" they may appear to the outsider.

It is easy to explain intellectually the Japanese *"way"* to Westerners, including those who have had absolutely no experience with Japan. But it is virtually impossible to transfer full understanding and appreciation of such behavior to someone else. The understanding has to be emotional and psychical to really make sense and be accepted. This means it has to be absorbed in real-life over a long period of time.

Western businessmen are constantly asking Japanese and others who are knowledgeable about Japan to tell them in a few minutes all they need to know to deal effectively with their Japanese counterparts. Such instant insights can help, but they can also be so superficial they do more harm than good.

In fact, much of the advice and counsel being given to Western politicians, diplomats and businessmen about how to deal with the Japanese covers only surface things and is often misleading because it creates false images and expectations that are not likely to materialize.

The recommended kata approach is to have expert counsel in all phases of a project/relationship throughout its lifetime and to *follow* advice when it comes from a genuine authority. When you do not have access to expert advice and must proceed without it, apologize (an acceptable kata) and do it your way, as diplomatically and courteously as you know how.

Westerners interested in absorbing some of the philosophy and psychic conditioning that makes up the Japanese way, without going to Japan, could consider taking up one or more of the country's martial arts, such as kendo and karate.

BEHIND-THE-SCENES MANAGEMENT

One of the most significant characteristics of Japanese management in larger companies and organizations, whether they are political, economic or business, is that the people out in front—those who appear to be the leaders—generally have limited authority and often no power at all.

There are a number of factors involved in this way of doing things, including the well-established consensus process of decision-making which diffuses responsibility to the point that it disappears and generally precludes the possibility of one man running the show.

Often just as important as the consensus factor is the well-established Japanese penchant for controlling things from behind the scenes—a cultural device that has been sanctified by nearly a thousand years of constant use. One of the earliest examples was Emperor Shirakawa who went into retirement in A.D. 1086, but continued to exercise power through fronts and agents.

Emperor Shirakawa was able to avoid the time-and-energy-concerning ceremonial aspects of power and management, giving himself a great deal more privacy and time to contemplate and maneuver. He could also manipulate people and events to a far greater extent than if he was required to do so publicly. And, finally, he was able to avoid all responsibility for any of his plans or actions that failed.

With this Imperial precedent of *insei* (een-say-e), or "secret life," it gradually became commonplace for Japanese leaders in all areas of business and life to "retire" early while continuing to manage events from the "closet."

Unfortunately, there was a fatal weakness in this system of indirect management that contributed to Imperial power being totally usurped as early as 1185 by military dictators who, in turn, were to be plagued by the same custom for the next seven hundred years.

The insei system, only slightly modified, still exists in modern Japan and is particularly conspicuous in politics where not one but several key figures control most power from behind the scenes, often with disastrous results, as witnessed by a number of scandals in the late 1980s.

One of the primary weaknesses of the insei system as practiced in Japan today is that it does not lend itself to a quick analysis and reaction to situations, and does not permit effective power to be focused on specific problems. This puts the Japanese government at a serious disadvantage in today's fast-moving world, particularly where its international relations and international events are concerned.

While the insei system has been very detrimental to Japan because it hides and protects the sources of power from public scrutiny and responsibility, it nevertheless has been very effective as a short-term weapon against foreign interests in both the political and economic sphere.

Probably the most notorious historical example of the insei factor occurred during the early 1800s when the U.S. and other European nations began attempting to establish diplomatic and trade relations with Japan. It was decades before Westerners realized that the emperor in Kyoto was powerless, and that the country was governed by a military dictatorship headquartered in Edo, as Tokyo was then called.

A great deal of time and effort were wasted during these decades because Westerners were not addressing the real power center. Even after the Edo-based shogunate government was identified, the problem of effective communication and negotiation was not resolved because authority and responsibility were so diffused.

This system allowed the Japanese government to delay its reaction to the foreign approaches and to design its eventual responses to suit its own purposes, not those of the foreign powers. This was to remain both the policy and the practice of the Japanese government as well as major business enterprises up to the present time.

Dealing with the Japanese government or a large commercial enterprise today is very much like trying to grasp and pin the arms of an octopus that keeps itself surrounded by a semi-opaque cloud of cultural smoke.

INTER-COMPANY RELATIONS

Inter-company relations in Japan are also kata-ized in keeping with the overall formal nature of traditional etiquette. Business between companies is not done on a simple company-to-company basis. It is primarily done on a people-to-people basis, meaning that personal and human relations have to be established with the appropriate managers before any transaction can occur.

Although the stricter requirements for first establishing personal relations with new firms have diminished significantly in recent decades, it is still common for managers to refuse to do business with companies they would *like* to sell to or buy from because the "proper relationship" does not exist. The first challenge in doing business with any Japanese company is for middle and upper level managers to establish the necessary personal ties on which trust and confidence are based.

Establishing such relationships invariably requires numerous meetings inside and outside of the company, with eating and drinking together playing a key role in the process. In fact, Japanese businessmen generally do not feel comfortable with anyone until they have gotten "drunk" together—the rationale being that you cannot really get to know people until all their defenses and facades are down and their true "heart" is revealed. In Japan strict etiquette prevents this from happening except during after hours drinking sessions.

The first kata in approaching a Japanese company is to go in with an introduction, preferably from someone they know personally and respect or are strongly obligated to—such as their banker, a key supplier or customer, etc. Introductions from important government agencies also carry weight.

All of the other company-to-company kata involve one or more facets of the etiquette system—from exchanging name-cards to making courtesy calls on special occasions (especially at the beginning of each new year), giving gifts when appropriate, and fulfilling a variety of social/personal obligations that come with building and sustaining the kind of relationship that is required in Japan to begin and to continue doing business.

Whether or not individuals or companies in Japan have established relationships generally determines the ethics of any contact between them. If there is no established relationship there is no specific obligation to treat the other party fairly (in the Western sense). In other words, Japanese tend to be "fair" only to those with whom they have on-going, desirable relationships. Since fairness in the form of equal treatment and equal opportunity for all is the bedrock of American ethics, Japanese and Americans often find themselves at loggerheads.

Foreign businessmen who expect to be treated fairly by Japanese companies without first having established a good, working relationship are more likely to be treated as adversaries who are "fair" game.

ADVANTAGES OF ILLOGICAL THINKING

One of the most conspicuous characteristics of the traditional Japanese Way is that they are conditioned to think in what might be described as circular or holistic terms rather than in the narrow straight lines that are favored in the West.

When viewed from the Western standpoint Japanese

thinking and behavior often appear irrational. In reality, however, the Japanese way of thinking and acting just as often turns out to be more rational, more logical than the Western way because the Japanese approach is more comprehensive, since it takes illogical as well as contradictory factors into consideration.

The fact that the traditional cultural mind-set of the Japanese is based in significant part on the ambiguities as well as the seeming contradictions of life has turned out to be one of their greatest strengths in dealing with the growing complexities of the modern world.

It would appear that one of the most conspicuous and vital advantages the ambiguity-minded Japanese have is their attitude and approach toward computer science. Rather than base their approach only on the off-on, black-white logic favored by Aristotelian conditioned American and European computer scientists, the Japanese were also quick to use the so-called "fuzzy logic" approach.

Japanese were not the first to conceive and develop the concept of fuzzy logic in programming computers. That was primarily the work of American scientists, but the mainstream of American and European computer scientists were philosophically opposed to "fuzzy thinking" and tended to ignore its validity and potential.

This cultural failure of the Western scientific community allowed Japanese scientists to become leaders in the practical application of holistic computer logic. By 1990 dozens of major Japanese companies (with government support) were using fuzzy logic to achieve far more precise and adaptable control of robots and a wide variety of appliances and electronic equipment—from subway systems to air-conditioning—than their Western counterparts who were just beginning to play catch-up.

It is ironic that one of the kata-ized Japanese traits that has been most criticized by Westerners has turned out to be one of Japan's strongest assets in competing with the rest of the world.

DESIGNING AS A CULTURAL EXPRESSION

For nearly one hundred years the Japanese were known to the West primarily as product copiers, a role that had been culturally required of them for nearly two thousand years. The kata of copying was transmitted to each new generation through a pervasive, long-term apprentice system that made each workman or craftsman a thorough-going professional in duplicating products and meeting quality standards that had been developed and mastered by past generations.

There was very little innovation or inventiveness in Japan during the long feudal period (1192-1868). In fact, the kata system worked against change and the political system often made change undesirable if not illegal. Once Japan had achieved a minutely defined political, economic and etiquette system the culture became relatively static. The concept of *kai zen* (kigh zen) or "continual improvement," for which Japanese industry is now world famous, is a very recent addition to the Japanese Way.

It was not until the 1950s that the Japanese became really free to introduce kai zen—to utilize their skills in designing new products or redesigning old ones to suit their tastes. Freed from centuries of political, economic and social repression, they brought an extraordinary amount of energy, direction and aesthetic ability to the challenge of designing new things.

There were no taboos, no ingrained mental blocks, about

how things should look, and some of their earliest designs—in shoes for example—were bizarre to Western eyes. But their culturally conditioned aesthetic sense and physical skills plus their propensity to humanize ordinary utilitarian things quickly came to the f ore. Within a decade the Japanese were known worldwide for both the quality and design of their products.

The special design ability of the Japanese is also a product of their kata-ized culture, beginning with their writing system and including their handicrafts and their traditional formalized etiquette, all of which are learned and transmitted by specific kata.

Training that all Japanese receive as part of their basic education, and the feel for form and order they develop as part of becoming Japanese, gives them the sensitivity and many of the fundamental skills so important to the creation of new, attractive, useful products. Until very recently almost every Japanese had the eye of an artist and a significant percentage of the population had the hand of an artist as well.

In 1958, I predicted that Japanese fashion designers would conquer the world within ten years. I was optimistic. The conquest did not happen but they are in the front ranks and still gaining momentum. Product designers in other categories are doing just as well.

PRODUCTION AS A
RELIGIOUS EXPERIENCE

Japan's success in productivity is emblazoned on the skylines of the world and is visible in virtually every home on the planet. The reason why Japan achieved such a high rate of productivity in such a short period of time (besides free access to the markets of the U.S. and

Europe and other external factors such as other people's wars and short-sighted policies) was because of its kata-ized culture, including everything from the principle of wa or harmony to groupism and self-sacrifice of the individual for the whole.

Japanese obsession with processes, their post-1950 "religion" of kai zen, or striving continuously to improve everything they make, and their equally powerful obsession to be number one in the world (because mastery is the ultimate purpose of every kata) fueled their spirit and their energy.

PACKAGING MAKES PERFECT

Superior design and productivity are not the only things that distinguish Japanese industry. Japanese packaging is also superior, and approached or equaled by only a few other countries.

Reasons for the packaging superiority of the Japanese include their cultural emphasis on aesthetics and their skill in translating their highly refined sense of harmony and beauty into everything from boxes to wrapping paper. Many of Japan's traditional forms of packaging, made of bamboo, other beautiful woods or handmade paper, are themselves works of handicraft art.

Not surprisingly, the Japanese are just as discriminating about packaging as they are about the products they contain. Product packaging must not only be right, when it is sold it must be wrapped and tied in the right way to satisfy the innate expectations of the Japanese. For a variety of things that are wrapped or enclosed there is a specific kind of string or cord that is required. Substituting some other kind of string would not only be a glaring error, it would result in a strong emotional reaction from the recipient. If a classy store committed such an oversight its whole image would suffer.

Foreign businessmen trying to sell consumer products in Japan learn very quickly that packaging can be as important as the product, just as the presentation of food in Japan is given as much importance as taste.

SEEING KATA IN ACTION

Visitors or new residents who want to see one of the most impressive—and important—demonstrations of kata in Japan have only to go a Mitsukoshi, Matsuzakaya or Takashimaya department store (or any other leading department store) just before the opening hour of 10 a.m. and enter the store the moment it opens.

At Mitsukoshi's Ginza branch in Tokyo, uniformed staff can be seen through the large plate-glass doors and windows making final preparations for the opening. At approximately one minute before the hour strikes, a braided rope is removed from the handles of the center doors. All of the doors have already been unlocked and the rope on the center door is just a sign that the store is not yet officially open.

As soon as the rope is removed staff members take up positions to the sides of each of the half dozen doors and stand at attention, forming the kind of receiving line associated with very formal occasions. By coincidence, a huge clock on the tower of the Wako Department Store across the street begins tolling loudly ten seconds before the hour. There is a dramatic build-up. At exactly 10 a.m., in perfect timing with the tolling bell of the clock, the staff in the receiving line bows in unison as a signal that the waiting customers may enter.

All floor personnel, mostly attractive women, are at

166

their stations, trimly uniformed and standing at attention. Managers are positioned at key areas on each floor. Additional staff, often including the floor managers, are stationed at the escalator landings on each floor. All bow and call out *Irasshaimase* (ee-rah-shy-ee-mah-say!)—"Welcome!"—to customers who come close to them. Managers often call out *Ohaiyo gozaimasu!* (Oh-high-yoe go-zie-mahss)—"Good Morning"—as well as "welcome."

It is an impressive example of the form and order—the kata—of the Japanese way and is indicative of the care and thoroughness with which the Japanese do things. The kata visible in the department store radiate feelings of efficiency, confidence, trust and security—all of which are part of the reason why most foreigners who visit Japan are so enamored of this aspect of the culture.

Just visiting a department store is often enough for first-time visitors to say, "Now I understand why the Japanese are so successful!"

Many Japanese companies are even more representative of traditional kata-ized behavior in modern settings. Visiting Konishi Sake Brewing Company in Itami (between Osaka and Kobe), makers of the famed Snow White brand of sake for fifteen generations, is like stepping back in time. The public areas of the huge traditionally styled headquarters building are furnished and decorated with impeccable aesthetic taste reflecting the arts and crafts of old Japan. Employees conduct themselves with ceremonial politeness, treating visitors with a refined etiquette that Westerners associate with old-style royalty. The atmosphere exudes competence, confidence, quality and a serene wisdom.

A week after my visit to Konishi I was greeted with exactly the same etiquette when visiting the corporate headquarters of Kikkoman in Tokyo, a firm especially noted for its internationalized policies and practices. This would seem to indicate that there is indeed a movement in Japanese companies to rejuvenate (or resurrect) traditional kata-ized behavior among their employees.

One of the most conspicuous examples of the continuing efficiency of Japan's kata-ized system is the amazing promptness of its commuter and long-distance trains. The famed "bullet trains" in particular are as precise as finely tuned watches—departing and arriving on the second.

This kind of absolute attention and dedication to detail and efficiency are among the characteristic attributes that Japanese owe to the kata factor in their culture—and will sorely miss if too many of the kata disappear.

5

WEAKNESSES OF THE JAPANESE SYSTEM

THE NEW PLAYING FIELD

Japan's remarkable kata culture has traditionally had its weaknesses as well as its strengths. As long as the country was isolated from the rest of the world, the inherent failings of the system were mostly kept submerged below the surface. Japanese were conditioned to accept the negative aspects of their behavior formulas, sacrificing their individuality and independence on the altar of harmony and the national polity.

An American businessman who had lived in Japan since

the mid-1950s and is bilingual, pinpointed one of the primary weaknesses of Japan's kata-ized system. He said: "In today's Japan the playing field is changing constantly while the kata remain the same. In traditional, isolated Japan the kata served as specific, absolute guidelines for all behavior. Now they are often a trap that regularly leads the Japanese over the edge."

He further commented that the Japanese turned kata-ized behavior into a ritual, and as a ritual it was unassailable. "How could a behavior be 'wrong' if it was sanctified ritual? To the Japanese of feudal Japan—and still to a considerable degree—life was ritual and ritual was life. That is the truest form of psychopathic behavior." Donald Richie, the noted analogist and writer, has observed that "Japaneseness" is often a neurotic symptom.

Still today when their behavior is challenged the Japanese frequently say, in so many words, "Don't question our behavior. You are criticizing the rituals that make us what we are! You must understand and accept us the way we are!"

Asking and expecting the Japanese to change their cultural stripes does, of course, represent a threat to the things they hold most sacred and vital to their identity. However, they recognize that they must change and must also make much more of an effort to understand the rest of the world. This means they must repudiate some of their most cherished ways.

At the same time, most Japanese are not aware of why they do what they do, or what they might be missing because of conformity to the Japanese Way. Most of them are absorbed by their kata mentality and continue to emphasize its strong points as the ultimate social formula which the rest of the world should adopt. Some of the most vehement

Japanese criticism I have ever heard of the American way of doing things was couched in terms of kata—in this case, the fact that Americans have no discernible kata in much of their behavior.

But with growing exposure to other cultures, more and more Japanese are beginning to realize that they live in a kind of kata-ized fishbowl; that their society is ruled by form and formulas and in a sense, in many areas, is empty of the individual human content that makes up a much more complete and satisfying emotional and spiritual life. Such persons are beginning to question the traditional cultural values, and to break the molds of the past.

One way of grasping the ongoing importance and role of kata-ized attitudes and manners in the lives of most Japanese, however, is to view the overall system as a minutely detailed and pervasive religious cult in which both the thinking and behavior of the members are prescribed and the system—at least in formal and business situations—is enforced with military sternness.

While the feudal laws of Japan have long since disappeared and the cult-like behavior that was demanded of all Japanese is now far more relaxed, most Japanese continue to exhibit traditional values and behavior to a degree that distinguishes them from all other national groups.

Iki-kata (ee-kee-kah-tah), or "way of living/' might have been called the master or mother kata of Japan in earlier times, when the way of living of each individual was clearly determined by social class, occupation and other specific factors. Within these feudal categories the way of living was basically prescribed, and enforced by group consensus and peer pressure as well as by law.

Japanese were programmed to know and follow the

style of living that was established for their *bun* category and status. The various iki-kata were not subject to individual interpretation, and remained virtually unchanged from one generation to the next.

Remnants of this cultural conditioning are readily discernible in Japan today. People are acutely sensitive about iki-kata—theirs as well as that of others—and are continuously concerned and talking about it. Any member of a company or other group who lives in a way that is markedly different from the others endangers his or her standing with the group. It can be personally as well as professionally damaging to be conspicuously different from others in your own group.

Said one English-speaking Japanese female employee of a major company: "I am like an alien in a Japanese face who happens to speak Japanese. The people around me are always asking me why I am different, why I speak English, why I think and sometimes behave differently than what they do. It just drives them up the wall."

Conforming to the expected iki-kata is a serious strain on the Japanese because it is role-playing to an extreme degree. It is like living on a stage where one's performance is under constant surveillance and any failure in form, dialogue or tone of voice is seen as a serious character and personality weakness; as being un-Japanese and therefore unacceptable.

This factor is the source of a great deal of frustration and anguish in Japan today because more and more young people are attempting to express their own individuality, to deliberately be different front other people, especially the huge mass of stereotypical Japanese. Of course, as more of these young people succeed in breaking out of the iki-kata molds of the past, the less likely they will be to conform to other kata-ized facets of the Japanese system.

Disenchantment with the Japanese system goes beyond new-age teenagers. Labor Ministry statistics show that job-hopping among middle-aged men in major corporations, almost unheard of in the 1970s, is growing rapidly. Dissatisfaction with work and a greater sense of personal freedom has turned job-hopping from taboo to trend, said a Ministry spokesman. Even more compelling than job-hopping is the growing number of Japanese men who drop out of sight each year because of alienation from the nation's workaholic culture and from their families.

While the kata factor has helped preserve and sustain some of the arts of traditional Japan it has worked against the flowering of modern art where individual interpretation and flights of imagination are often keys to greatness. Critics say that the art world in Japan is so rigid and stifling that it produces artists who are technically polished but lacking in emotion and fire. This has resulted in droves of young musicians and painters fleeing Japan and establishing colonies abroad.

Because the life-style of Japan's younger generations is undergoing profound changes there is a conspicuous degree of apparent artificiality about much of the hybrid attitudes and forms that one now encounters. "Many people in Japan are no longer real", said one critic. "Japanese who speak English are faking it. Some of them cannot be real even in Japanese. They are faking it in both languages and cultures."

After Westerners began attaching growing significance to the distinctive Japanese way of doing things, particularly from the early 1970s on, the Japanese themselves gradually picked up on the theme and soon became even more fascinated than Westerners with their cultural traits. This led to a growing debate about whether or not Japan should give up its traditional culture in order to be more in tune with Western countries.

RIGHT-BRAIN VS. LEFT-BRAIN

Dozens of theories have been put forth by Japanese psychologists, sociologists, businessmen and others in an attempt to explain typical Japanese attitudes and behavior. Probably the most startling of these theories was one advanced by Dr. Tadanobu Tsunoda, formerly a lecturer in otology and audiology at the Tokyo Medical and Dental University (TMDU) and a professor at the Department of Auditory Disorders at the Medical Research Institute of TMDU.

Dr. Tsunoda, who published his theory in a book entitled *THE JAPANESE BRAIN—Uniqueness and Universality* (Taishukan Publishing Co., Tokyo), presented data which he said proved that the Japanese use their brains differently than other people, and that this difference accounts for the uniqueness of the Japanese way of thinking and acting.

Dr. Tsunoda attributes the uniqueness of the Japanese directly to their language. He says the Japanese *are Japanese* because they speak the Japanese language. The Japanese created the language in their own cultural image. Over the course of time, it became the primary medium of the culture, and helps to sustain it in a very direct way..

If I understand Dr. Tsunoda's thesis correctly, he believes that the prominence of vowels in the Japanese language causes the Japanese to perceive and interpret natural and manmade sounds differently than other people, resulting in fundamental differences in the way they think and behave. He says that this language difference results in the Japanese generally not distinguishing between reason and emotion because they process input on a different side of the brain, than most people. In fact, Dr. Tsunoda says the only other people in the world who think like the Japanese are Polynesians, whose language is also rich in vowels.

Without getting into the complicated details of Dr. Tsunoda's theory, the variety and number of obvious exceptions to it suggests very strongly that there is much more to Japan's unique culture than differences brought on by a characteristic of the language.

Like the famous Japanese frog in a well which could see only a speck of the universe, Dr. Tsunoda's view of the origin of the Japanese Way, as seen from the depths of his own cultural well, caused him to look in the wrong place for his answers. Since he could "see" nothing that accounted for the distinctive mind-set and behavior of the Japanese, he assumed it was caused by some internal physical factor and chose the Japanese brain as the source.

This may be the ultimate in wishful thinking by the Japanese, going well beyond such previous claims that Japanese skin, is different from the skin of other people (therefore foreign-made cosmetics are not suitable for Japanese); that Japanese intestines are longer than foreign intestines (and therefore certain imported foods are not appropriate for the Japanese); that since the Japanese do not understand themselves, there is no way foreigners can understand them, etc.

This is part of the great dilemma of the Japanese. They know they differ from other people in many cultural ways, and there is a strong cultural-driven compulsion to take pride in these differences and to glory in them. Yet there is also a yearning, especially among those born after 1950, to be "like" other national groups and to be accepted as "normal" by them.

I fully agree with Dr. Tsunoda's theory that the nature of the Japanese language is responsible for many distinctive features of Japanese culture. He proposes that the language, *when used in the Japanese way,* influences the patterns of thought and behavior of the Japanese. This seems indisputable, and I have long used key Japanese words in attempting to explain Japanese attitudes and actions.

Dr. Tsunoda goes beyond the idea of the language influencing the mental processes of the Japanese. He says that when the Japanese use or hear a foreign language, their brain shifts hemispheres, going from the right side, which he says is their normal operating mode, to the left side, because of basic differences in the sounds of the languages. When this automatic shift occurs, according to Dr. Tsunoda's theory, the Japanese are no longer able to think like Japanese and suddenly find themselves in an alien world.

Listening to and speaking a foreign language is thus a traumatic experience for the Japanese, adds Dr. Tsunoda, and the longer they remain in the left-brain (foreign) mode, the longer it takes for them to revert back to the Japanese mode and recover from the experience. In hearing-and-brain-activity response tests conducted on himself, Dr. Tsunoda said it took him approximately seven days to return to normal after participating in an English language conference.

He suggests that extensive exposure to foreign

languages can so befuddle the Japanese that their right-brain hemisphere is short-circuited, preventing them from being able to think creatively. This does not appear to be the case in practical application, however, since many of Japan's most creative thinkers and innovators speak some English and are regularly exposed to its sounds.

Furthermore, it is technically possible for anyone, including the Japanese, to speak the Japanese language in a very non-Japanese way. When foreigners speak Japanese in a non-Japanese way the Japanese more or less expect it. They often do not approve of it but they are not shocked by it. If, on the other hand, a Japanese speaks the language in a "foreign" way, especially in business and other formal or semi-formal situations, it is totally unacceptable and unforgivable. If the speaker persists in using the language in a non-Japanese manner he is ostracized.

Whether Dr. Tsunoda's theory is right or wrong, it is in line with the observations of one foreign linguist, quoted earlier, who says that the Japanese have a tendency to regard what they say in English or any other foreign language as unreal, as having no bearing on what they really think or believe, and may therefore not be binding.

This suggests that all of Japan's international affairs, business as well as diplomatic, should be—or must be—conducted in Japanese, otherwise any true meeting of the minds is virtually impossible. The fact that most foreign dialogue with Japan is not and never has been conducted in Japanese suggests the immensity of the problem. Much of the friction between Japan and the rest of the world is, of course, the result of inadequate and failed communications—of the Japanese and foreign sides speaking on different frequencies.

Probably the most common example of miscommunication between Japanese and foreigners results from the reluctance of the Japanese to say "no" clearly and unequivocally. There are half a dozen or more expressions that are commonly used to express the negative but mislead foreigners who fail to translate them properly. Typically when a Japanese says "I will think it over" they mean "I'm not interested." When they say something is "difficult" they mean it cannot be done. When they say "I will do my best" they mean what you are asking for is impossible and you might as well forget it.

THE DOWNSIDE OF SPEAKING JAPANESE

There is another aspect of foreign language communication in Japan that plays a significant role in relationships between foreigners and Japanese. It often happens that speaking Japanese well or fairly well can be more of a disadvantage than a help. This situation occurs when the Japanese concerned react by treating the foreign speaker as a Japanese rather than as a foreigner—the point being that the Japanese tend to be more accommodating, hospitable and lenient toward foreigners than they are to other Japanese.

Most foreigners in Japan pick up on this Japanese peculiarity very quickly/ and some develop considerable skill at using it to their advantage. Some also use the characteristics of the language as a rationale for not making any serious attempt to learn it.

Says a bilingual foreign businessman, "Japanese is a 'loaded' language in the sense that when you speak it you are expected to act Japanese. Therefore when I want to be direct and demanding, I use English. I also find English useful when I want to make it difficult for the other party to make an excuse. When I want to be vague, I use Japanese. This has nothing to do with the nature of the language. The exact same logical thought can be constructed in Japanese and English in more or less the same number of words, but if delivered in Japanese it will sound more direct, and often rude."

There are apparently a number of reasons why the Japanese often react more positively to English than they do to their own language—even when their English is so poor that any conversation with them is awkward and frustrating. This response apparently derives from an overwhelming desire to practice their English, to demonstrate their international ability, or to accommodate the foreigner. It is also common for the Japanese to automatically presume that foreigners do not speak Japanese—and sometimes to ignore the fact when they do. Which of these reasons is paramount depends on the individual.

The Japanese image of foreigners as not being able to speak Japanese, as outsiders who cannot come to know or become Japanese under any circumstances, and therefore as temporary visitors regardless of their status in Japan, results in them tending to regard all foreigners more or less as "guests." As guests they are generally accorded special treatment.

Speaking English (or other foreign languages) helps keep foreigners in the "foreign guest" category and allows them to presume on the special treatment the Japanese typically lavish on visitors. Their mistakes and mishaps are commonly indulged to a remarkable degree, and individual Japanese will often go out of their way to help foreigners.

Allowing and/or encouraging the Japanese to speak English, even though you may speak their language, can go well beyond the guest treatment syndrome if you know what you are doing and can control the situation. As Dr. Tsunoda says, Japanese think and behave differently when functioning in English. Their kata-ized ways do not carry over. The degree of the cultural change that occurs depends on the individual's ability in the foreign language as well as on his or her knowledge and experience with the foreign culture in general.

When foreigners are able to communicate with the Japanese in English the communication may be complete insofar as the individual Japanese is concerned. But how effective the English-speaking Japanese can be in communicating the same understanding to non-English speaking co-workers or others is another matter. Problems arise when the foreign side expects too much from English-speaking Japanese— who have their own set of handicaps when communicating with other Japanese.

Generally speaking, the deliberate use of English to draw the Japanese out of their cultural shell and take advantage of the guest syndrome is usually effective in relatively minor situations where single individuals are concerned. But in important matters concerning several people, regardless of the subject, it is much more likely to be ineffective and to be dangerous if not fatal, especially if only one or two on the Japanese side speak English. The foreigner typically goes away thinking he has made his point and it has been accepted, while the non-English speaking Japanese are likely to be confused, frustrated or antagonistic.

SPEAKING IN TONGUES

Another piece of evidence that the Japanese language is

not responsible for the attitudes and actions of the Japanese is that there appears to be absolutely nothing sacred about the language. It is chopped, diced and blended to fit the mood or needs of the speaker. The formal language taught in schools is not what you hear out in the real world. New words, usually adapted from English, are added almost daily—and usually make no sense at all to either Japanese or English speakers until they are broken down and carefully explained.

It is apparently official Japanese government policy that certain topics that are likely to be viewed negatively by the public are referred to in Japanized English words. The advertising industry also regularly introduces new made-up words. The role and importance of new words in Japan is indicated by the annual "Japan New Words & Popular Words Awards/' sponsored by the publishing firm Jiyu Kokumin-sha, publishers of the annual Basic Information and Current Technology dictionary.

The winning word in the New Words division in last year's contest was *sekusharu harashimento*$_L$ pronounced "say-kuu-shah-rue hah-rah-she-mane-toe" (sexual harassment). My all-time favorite is *bum baado* or buu-rue bah-doe (blue bird), a popular car model. When this name was first introduced one of my friends, who already knew what it meant, left me puzzled for hours, trying to figure out what it referred to. Another of my favorites is *kosu meto* (koe-sue may-toe), which means "course mate," and refers to female golf caddies. Keeping up with the changing times in Japan is an unending language lesson that often amuses as well as befuddles.

Both doctors and marketers in Japan do attest that the Japanese read and process Kan-Ji on the right side of their brains, whereas phonetic writing—such as English—is processed and stored in the left side of the brain. This is apparently the reason why the Japanese (and other Orientals who use Kan-Ji) have a greater ability to perceive and use symbols, which are now most commonly seen in advertising.

CHANNELING COMPETITIVE POWER

University of Tokyo social scientist Takeshi Ishida disagrees with Dr. Tsunoda's left-right brain theories about Japanese behavior. He attributes the distinctive behavior of the Japanese to what he calls "the integration of conformity and competition." In his scenario, conformity of the highest order is achieved through the creation and maintenance of specific groups.

Within each Japanese group, members compete fiercely against each other to continuously prove their loyalty to the group and to contribute to its growth, thereby making the group dynamic instead of static. Each group in turn competes just as fiercely against all other groups.

This competitive powered conformity not only generates tremendous energy, says Professor Ishida, it also makes it possible for the Japanese to effect abrupt changes in their attitudes and behavior because the moment a group demands a new attitude, competitive loyalty within the conformity-oriented group takes over and the members outdo themselves to conform to the new demands.

Professor Ishida notes, however, that there is both a positive and a negative side to Japan's competitive conformity within groups. On the positive side the system provides for the resolution of intra-group friction and conflicts by compromise (because they threaten its existence), and it ensures that the group will act together as a single unit when threatened from the outside.

The major weakness of groups bound together by competitive loyalty, continues Professor Ishida, is that the system virtually eliminates the possibility of any member of the group taking individual responsibility of any kind. Another weakness is that once a group sets out on a particular course of action it is extremely difficult to stop the action, even when it turns out to be wrong or detrimental to the group and the group becomes aware of it.

Professor Ishida says that the origin of the elements making up Japan's conformity in a closed in-group system can be traced directly to the village system that existed from earliest times. From the beginning of Japan's history, most of its villages existed in virtual isolation from each other because of the country's myriad mountain ranges, as well as numerous political divisions. In the early 1600s the newly established Tokugawa shogunate passed edicts forbidding residents from moving out of their villages, thus institutionalizing the closed in-groups that were already common to rural communities.

With the downfall of the Tokugawa regime in 1868, the new Meiji government continued to limit the movement of people from villages, apparently to prevent exposure to civil rights movements outside of the villages, and went to great lengths to adopt the in-group conformity and competition, system of the villages in government on both a local and national level.

As the primary sponsor of the industrialization of Japan from 1868 on, the Meiji government strongly backed the concept of all companies also being managed as family or "village" enterprises in a system that was quickly institutionalized under rigid bureaucratic leadership. Smaller enterprises were operated very much like single family units; larger companies like villages.

National conformity in Japan was strengthened by a universal education system that emphasized group spirit and harmony above all other considerations. Mass news media that: appeared following the downfall of the Tokugawa shogunate became an additional force in homogenizing the Japanese mind-set in the values of the Japanese Way. The only news readers got was what the media managers and government censors felt would protect and strengthen national goals. Given the nature of the traditional in-group values, the Japanese saw every outsider as a threat.

Since social and economic harmony was the primary aim of Japan's village group system, it was necessary to control competition by defining it in terms of the group. The only practical way this could be done was for competition to be expressed in terms of loyalty to the group. Each member was expected to do his best to prove his loyalty. In present-day Japan, this constant striving to prove loyalty incorporates the individual's immediate group, the company and finally the nation. Success in Japan comes primarily from proving one's group loyalty as opposed to individual accomplishment, and, by extension, from proving one's Japanese-ness.

JAPAN ON "CLARK'S CURVE"

The most provocative theory so far advanced by Western scholars to explain the Japaneseness of the Japanese was probably Jochi (Sophia) University Professor Gregory Clark's so-called "Clark Curve." Professor Clark said the

Japaneseness of the Japanese was directly attributable to their current stage of psychological/intellectual development from emotional, instinctive principles to logical, rationalistic principles.

Professor Clark related this developmental process to instinctive values found in early village societies, and the gradual appearance of rational values as each society goes through successive stages of feudalism and industrialization. He said Japan was well behind Europe, America and the Middle East on this curve of economic and social progress.

On Dr. Clark's "curve" he showed Japan as approaching the peak of the arc, which represents the ideal between instinctive values and rational values. He said that Europe, America and some other older countries were on the down side of the curve, where motivations are primarily selfish and aimed at personal gain rather than achieving a mutually cooperative spirit and system that benefits all.

Dr. Clark's curve theory may provide a possible framework for understanding and measuring personal and social values in a society, but it does not answer the question of "what makes a Japanese?" or explain the whys of specific Japanese attitudes and behavior.

All societies are no doubt somewhere on the Clark Curve, but none are, or have been, exactly like the Japanese, including Koreans and Chinese whose values and customs most closely resemble those of Japan. The answer to the question, "What is a Japanese?" is both far more sophisticated and specific than where they may be on logic versus instinct curve.

In the 1980s the Japanese were forever asking foreigners if they didn't believe that the Japanese were *hen* (hane)—which means "strange," with decidedly negative connotations. 1 was asked this question dozens of times in 1949 when I first went to Japan and was asked the same question over four decades later aboard a plane about to arrive in Los Angeles from Tokyo.

The thirty-year-old Tokyo businessman who was the last person to ask me if I thought the Japanese were *hen* struggled valiantly to find a word that would describe what the Japanese wanted to be like (instead of being the way they perceive themselves to be), and he finally said: "We want to be continental!"

That was the first time I had heard the yearning of the Japanese expressed in this term, and I was delighted with the sense and style of it. How absolutely appropriate, I thought.

All things considered the Japanese have changed remarkably fast—especially so, given the scope, power and exclusivity of their culture. But on a practical day-to-day basis, particularly in politics and business, the changes are often difficult to discern. Frustrated foreign residents in Japan as well as many Japanese often say the Japanese are changing for the worse instead of the better—in some cases meaning they are becoming more *Japanese* in the traditional sense.

There is no denying that as the force of the traditional kata weakens, the Japanese character is changing in ways that are already having a significantly negative impact on their society—juvenile crime and rampant materialism being among the most conspicuous of the changes.

WAVES IN THE WORLD OF WA

While Japan's business facade generally presents a world of wa (harmony) in excellent if not perfect working order, reality is often quite different. In many companies there are overriding conflicts of interest among the section and department managers as each tries to outdo or out-maneuver the other to stay on the corporate escalator that carries them toward the limited number of top executive posts.

Competition for promotion to the higher levels within a company often results in Machiavellian political intrigue that impacts on the attempts of outsiders to do business with these companies. Projects often fail, regardless of their merit, because of opposition from section or department managers seeking their own advantage or to block the advantage of someone else.

This political infighting within many Japanese companies follows patterns of kata set down generations ago. It is usually manifested in the behavior of groups, made up of either sections *(ka)* or departments *(bu)*, who conspire to advance their own programs at the expense of others.

The kata-ized group system protects and sustains itself by acting more or less as a single-cell unit. The chief regularly takes credit for the brilliant ideas or accomplishments of underlings, knowing that he can maintain their loyalty and support because they are not likely to quit, cannot be promoted over him, and because they depend upon him to pull them along with him as he ascends the organizational ladder.

This system creates a facade of order and harmony that is often an illusion. It also contributes to the relative immobility of labor among Japan's top companies because it is virtually impossible for an individual to be accepted in a new group except at the bottom when young and at the top when old. There are a specific number of slots in a group, each with its own ranking. No one wants to be shoved aside or pushed down by a newcomer.

Another key factor in the kata-ized mentality of Japanese management is intolerance toward anyone who does not play the game according to the rules of the system. Deviations from the norm are not written down, but they become a permanent part of the individual's "record." A manager who makes this kind of cultural mistake is typically shunted off of the promotion escalator, and thereafter is moved sideways instead of up.

One of the more serious "mistakes" a manager can make in a tradition-bound Japanese company is to show too much independence and individuality, to achieve successes on his own and accept credit for them. The "proper" way is for him to maintain a very humble manner and credit everyone except himself.

The combination of exclusive group orientation and the vertical structure of traditional Japanese companies—the classic pyramid organization—often results in very poor communication between the departments within companies, inability to delegate authority, and very slow response time—all factors that foreign businessmen must contend with when dealing with Japanese firms.

The more internationalized a Japanese company, the more likely it is to have a so-called *bunchin* (booncheen) or "paperweight" structure. The connotation here is that the organizational system of the bunchin company has been flattened (as paper is flattened by a paperweight) to make the flow of communication easier.

Japanese critics of the pyramid system of organization say such companies cannot convert to the bunchin system until they develop a clear-cut philosophy, an equally clear company policy, learn how to delegate authority, and develop skills in communicating—all cultural factors that respond slowly to changing times.

PERSONAL FAILINGS

Viewed from the outside the Japanese often appear to be caricatures of their culture; stick-figures who can think and behave only in one way—a way that was programmed into them from infancy by rote conditioning. This impression is probably wrong as often as it is right, but the cultural programming still undergone by most Japanese makes it difficult and sometimes impossible for them to cope in a foreign environment.

An arbitrary listing of the "typical" Japanese weaknesses the Japanese themselves used to bring up included:

1) Inability to think and act independently
2) Inability to take the lead in most situations
3) A tendency to think in terms of absolute stereotypes
4) Stereotyping everyone in terms of family, education, university, company, company-size, and position
5) A tendency to maintain the status quo until pressured from the outside
6) A tendency to do nothing rather than cause any kind of friction
7) Withholding facts pertaining to a situation at hand
8) Rarely saying what they really think

9) Rarely volunteering a direct opinion
10) Invoking their Japaneseness as justification for their attitudes and behavior
11) Persistent small-mindedness
12) Almost no sense of reciprocity in a general context
13) Little regard for the privacy of others
14) An undeveloped sense of the rights of others
15) Inability to identify themselves with other nationalities and races
16) A growing impulsiveness, impatience and rudeness, especially in Tokyo
17) Growing arrogance

Historically, the Japanese educational and industrial training processes were based on copying and learning by repetition. Subject matter in schools was the same for everyone up through high school. Students learned by rote memorization. Variations in the process were not permitted. This system created a passive population conditioned to follow customs and orders, and worked against change and innovation.

This traditional learning and training process has weakened and is under heavy pressure to change further, but both the private and public lives of most Japanese remain in the grip of the kata system, and change—for good or bad—is slow. The biggest and perhaps most significant change in the system is that in some companies and organizations, group creativity has been given the highest possible priority, and individual creativity by maverick researchers and tinkerers is now tolerated in some areas.

Still, the kata-ized culture has given the Japanese a built-in reverence for rigidity that prevails in the face of all kinds of evidence that a flexible response would be more beneficial to them. This rigidity is still used for the sake of form, for harmony, and as a weapon to thwart the goals of competitors, particularly foreign interests.

MIGHT IS RIGHT

Another value that became a part of the national consciousness of the Japanese following its opening to the West in 1868 was that "might is right/" and that the domination of the weak by the strong is a natural organic process. This philosophy had existed in Japan since ancient times but it was given new life and scope by their observation of the Western colonial powers of the day and the importation of Darwin's survival of the fittest theory.

Generally speaking, the Japanese now feel superior to other people because of their extraordinary economic success. There is a tendency for the Japanese to look upon other people as not deserving of success because they are less disciplined and less educated than the Japanese, and are viewed as too lazy, materialistic or indifferent to help themselves. By extension, the Japanese tend to believe it is right and proper for them to exercise dominion over such people— attitudes and behavior that have historically been present in Western societies as well.

Because much of Japan's dynamism emanates from the energy of competitive loyalty within hundreds of thousands of core cells, where it works something like a nuclear chain reaction that feeds on its own success, deliberately slowing the juggernaut of Japan's economic expansion abroad in a short period of time is virtually impossible. Slowing it down over a long period of time can take place only in terms of fundamental changes in the culture. This means, of course, that rapid changes in Japan are not likely to occur without effective pressure from the outside.

As previously mentioned, Japanese tend to have a deep-seated dislike, even contempt, for weakness. Conversely they are impressed by strength, courage, strong will and unswerving dedication to personal and national goals. One of the factors now coloring their image of the United States is what they perceive as a fading of boldness and resolve and a growing "smell of weakness" in the American people.

This new attitude in Japan was expressed in a variety of ways. As one example, a Japanese educator of my acquaintance was among one of several influential people who advocated that Japan acquire a large area of the United States on a 99-year lease, and move several hundred thousand Japanese into the enclave as permanent residents. The Japanese "colonists" would then provide the long-range planning, management skills and energy seen as essential to reinvigorate the American economy.

CAN JAPAN SURVIVE WITHOUT KATA?

JAPAN VS. THE WORLD

Significant advances have been made by most Japanese in broadening their traditional attitudes, but one still constantly hears, especially among businessmen and politicians, that all of the trade friction and conflicts between

Japan and the rest of the world will disappear as soon as foreigners succeed in understanding the Japanese viewpoint. Of course, the very clear message is that these problems stem from the ignorance and intransigence of the foreign side, not from the attitudes and actions of the Japanese.

Despite the fact that the Japanese are at least partially correct in their view of their international political and trade relations, cultural handicaps make it difficult and sometimes impossible for them to achieve the understanding and cooperation from foreign countries they so ardently desire.

Some of the handicaps holding the Japanese back are exacerbated by their kata-ized conditioning in the Tightness and righteousness of the Japanese way, in groupism, in consensus decision-making, and so on. This puts the Japanese in a classic bind. Their kata culture is the main source of both their most enviable strengths *and* their most debilitating weaknesses.

How the Japanese handle this immediate dilemma will decide their future for generations to come.

THE DWINDLING KATA

Learning how to read and draw Kan-Ji, the Chinese characters with which the Japanese write their language, is no doubt one of the most important factors in the survival of Japan's traditional culture, but the overall influence of Kan-Ji is eroding rapidly. The number of characters the Japanese are required to learn in school was reduced from around five thousand to some two thousand in the 1950s.

The appearance of Japanese language typewriters, word-processors and computers in the 1970s and 1980s contributed to a further erosion of the role of kaki-kata or "way of writing" in the cultural conditioning of the Japanese. As more and more people switch from writing

Kan-Ji to key-boarding Kan-Ji, the weaker the kata of writing has become. Even the beautiful art of *shodo* (calligraphy) seems destined to become a victim of technology. A "calligraphy machine" called *fude gaki* (fuu-day gah-kee) or "brush writer," which makes it possible for anyone to mechanically print addresses and short messages in stylized brush strokes, was introduced in 1990.

Many high school graduates now have to take intensive refresher courses in reading and writing before they can hope to pass examinations to get into universities. Within a few years after leaving school a growing number of Japanese have forgotten how to write many of the less common Chinese characters, and some have forgotten how to read them as well. The tendency for publishers to more and more use the simplified phonetic writing systems, hira-gana and kata-kana, instead of the multi-stroke Kan-Ji, is rapidly gaining ground.

There appears to be no doubt that future users of computers will have a choice of activating them by voice and getting a verbal response, thus eliminating both the need for keyboarding and the ability to read Kan-Ji. This will further erode the power and influence of the kata culture.

In the same way that the introduction of streetcars and trains had a profound influence on the Japanese choice of wearing apparel as well as their public behavior in the late 1800s, changes in the practice and use of Kan-Ji today are inexorably changing Japan in subtle as well as conspicuous ways.

Just as the Japanese of the Meiji period could not freeze their stylized etiquette system within the type of constraints that existed during their earlier feudal era, present-day Japanese cannot prevent the further diminishing of their traditional way of writing. Other kata as well are slowly but inexorably losing their power. More importantly, the very young are no longer being thoroughly conditioned in the traditional cultural molds in their homes. The result is a fundamental weakening of the famed "Japanese Way."

Japan is now faced with the passing of its last fully kata-ized generation. Each year some five percent or so of the remaining "real" Japanese, those who were responsible for the country's extraordinary economic success, retire because of old age, or die off. Over half of them were gone by the year 2,000 and all of them will disappear from the scene in the following two decades.

This very rapid and very conspicuous disappearance of the "founding fathers" of present-day Japan, and their replacement by people who are regarded as a "new breed," as virtual aliens, is viewed by many as the most profound threat Japan has ever faced. Fear of what could happen to a de-Japanized Japan is the main force in driving the old generation of Japanese to create one last miracle before they die-the "internationalization" of Japanese culture and the economy.

Unfortunately, being "international" to most Japanese means little more than wearing Western style clothing, eating Western style food, traveling abroad, speaking a little English or some other foreign language, enjoying Western music, and having some interest in international affairs. It does not mean cultural or racial tolerance, economic reciprocity, or an open society.

INROADS OF WESTERNIZATION

The biggest immediate threat to Japan's overall kata culture is, of course, the mounting influence of Western ideas and customs. With time and distance virtually eliminated by technology and their national borders open to two-way travel and trade, the Japanese are being directly exposed to the world for the first time in their history. But they do not have an effective kata for handling this totally new experience, and are in a constant state of agitation.

Western influence washing over Japan is especially disruptive because it emphasizes individuality and personal responsibility. Westerners tend to accept individual responsibility and to be willing to take chances. Japanese society has traditionally spread responsibility within groups and cushioned the effects of failure, with the result that the Japanese are more wary of unpredictability and accepting responsibility than they are of failure.

Fear of unpredictability in Japan was, and still is, enormously strengthened by the power and influence of the kata. The smooth working of Japanese society is based on everyone following the accepted kata, as opposed to abstract principles which are always open to various interpretations. The subversion or flouting of proper form is therefore much more threatening to the Japanese than failing in any enterprise. Westerners and Western ways represent unpredictability to the Japanese.

One of the major challenges now facing the Japanese as the old kata-based culture weakens is to develop a tolerance for unpredictability and the ability to deal with it. This, of course, is much easier said than done, and it will probably be two or three generations before it becomes a significant part of the Japanese character—assuming they make the effort in the first place.

As Japan's kata culture weakens, the incidence of intimidation, assault, battery and other forms of violence is becoming more and more commonplace. Genuine wa (harmony) is already hard to find in the urban areas of the country. The Japanese are acutely aware that their kata-ized culture is breaking up. They understand the universal principle that progress comes only with change, but, unlike earlier historical occasions when great changes occurred, they are no longer able to control events from the top.

For a preview of what one side of Japan could be like without kata, all one has to do is turn on the television set and watch a number of the regular comedy shows. Veteran journalist Ronald E. Yates has described this facet of Japanese television as "the Kabuki-cho of Japan." Kabuki-cho is a district in West Tokyo that is notorious as the sleaze capital of the country. Yates was referring to the fact that several of the most popular of these shows are in turn vulgar, irreverent, pornographic, thoughtless, callous, even cruel.

The shows are immensely popular, apparently because the comedians break every kata-ized taboo in the system, thereby providing a vicarious release for their audiences.

Because they are no longer able to prevent changes in their social system and are no longer in full control of their economic system, the Japanese may very well be unable to survive at the present level—or at a higher level—without the benefit of a kata-ized population.

What the diminishing of just the Kan-Ji system alone means to Japan's future is, of course, open to conjecture, but there is no doubt that it will be a major factor in the de-traditionalizing of the culture and subsequently have a negative effect on the character and behavior as well as the abilities of the Japanese.

Kabuki is a good example of the ultimate in kata-izing human behavior, revealing not only its strengths in providing precise guidelines for each new performer to master the set form, but also the weakness and inhumanity of the system as well in that: it rejects any individuality or new intelligence and thus stifles change and growth of the person and the art.

Still the Japanese tend to look upon kabuki as representative of the best of traditional Japan, and continue to herd foreign visitors to the kabuki-za for a taste of the "real Japan" without realizing that they might also be showing the worst side of Japanese culture.

To the degree that an automated kind of behavior served Japan's needs, kata-ization was a remarkable way to mobilize energy and skill in achieving specific, set goals. But in those areas where flexibility, spontaneity and art must be one, the negative effects of some kata, when carried to the ultimate, are equally obvious—and frightening.

Overall, the kata system will probably continue to be the most important cultural influence in shaping the national character of the Japanese throughout the first quarter of the 21st century, carried forward not only by their spoken and written language but also by their daily etiquette, their aesthetic and martial arts and the prevailing educational and business systems.

Japan's educational system and its employment and management practices remain key factors in helping to sustain the traditional aspects of the culture—in direct opposition to other efforts to internationalize the country. Still today one of the most common sights in elementary schools in Japan is masses of young children, down on the floor, painting huge Kan-Ji characters on large sheets of paper. Many managers in larger Japanese companies are also deliberately trying to keep the kata culture alive because they recognize that despite its drawbacks it has been a key factor in the economic success of the country.

But both the educational and traditional management systems of Japan are under increasing pressure to change.

197

There is no doubt that the more "international" the Japanese become the more the influence of the kata system will weaken. The more they give up the cultural practices that made them a special and formidable nation the more of these special advantages they will lose.

The price the Japanese must pay to internationalize their society—in other words, become less Japanese and more like Westerners—is high, and there are many who feel it would not be worth it. Ideally, of course, the best solution would be for the Japanese to maintain, the kata that are positive and result in desirable attitudes and habits, and drop those that have proven to be harmful.

In any event it was too early to begin counting Japan out. Veteran *Japan Times* columnist Jean Pearce noted (just as American mariner Henry Holmes did in the mid-1800s) that the Japanese were still capable of surprising the world. In a "Getting Things Done" column written in the late 1980s, Pearce presented a list of changes that occurred in Japan in the previous five years that were hardly imaginable a decade earlier. These changes included Japanese attitudes and policies regarding conservation, recycling paper, banning the ivory trade, and preserving the environment in general.

Just as important, such changes in Japan are not the result of a totally new awareness. As Pearce also observed, more often than not they are a return to traditional values that were a fundamental part of Japanese culture for more than a thousand years. These old, familiar, resurrected traditions, like their kata heritage from the past, now constitute cultural advantages that are contributing to Japan's new role as a world leader.

It was not until the 1980s that Japanese business and government leaders began to systematically sponsor the export of Japanese culture on a large, coordinated scale. Given Japan's economic role in the world today this new effort is likely to be successful, based not so much on Japan's skill in exporting but on the growing motivation of foreign countries to be receptive to and often take the lead in importing Japanese ideas and processes in order to compete with Japan.

The study of the Japanese language around the world now rivals the study of English, and is doing more to spread Japanese culture than anything else. In fact, it was not until the latter part of the 1980s that Japanese leaders began to realize that it is primarily language—not kabuki, sushi, ramen noodles, cars or television sets—that transmits culture, and are now supporting this new, extraordinary phenomenon.

WILL THE JAPANESE REMAIN NO. 3?

One of the kata-bound cultural forces that has traditionally driven the Japanese is the need to excel in everything— to do things better and to achieve more than other people. This compulsive drive is evident in virtually everything they do. Generally speaking, the superlative is their ultimate goal, whether it is the smallest, the largest, the highest, the most durable, the finest in quality or whatever.

This built-in need often manifests itself in what could be described as a national psychosis. A recent typical example: a marathon runner who failed to live up to national expectations in an international meet was criticized vehemently and received a number of death threats.

The origin of this psychosis is no doubt the perfection demanded by every kata in Japan's cultural system. Kata goals are unbounded, and carry over into all areas of life. Thus kata-ized Japanese cannot be satisfied with being anything but first or best. This compulsion goes beyond

199

common nationalistic feelings, playing a particularly key role in international business because that is linked with economic well-being. It also leads some Japanese to envision Japan as the world's paramount economic power.

Most thinking Japanese routinely denied that Japan had aspirations of being No. 1 in the world. Commentators in many fields regularly noted that they (meaning all Japanese) were perfectly happy to be No. 2. Besides, they add, there is no conceivable way Japan *could* be first. By the 1980s, however, other Japanese began speculating that not only could Japan become the world's top economic power, there was, in fact, a good chance that it would—as much by default as by its own efforts.

But growing indications that Japan might indeed become No. 1 in the world's economic order were frightening to most Japanese. They believed such success would turn the world against them and they would once again be isolated. Even the most passionate expansionists were acutely aware that it is too early for them to openly seek the primary leadership role in the world. Yet there were some who were preparing for that day.

The world at large can take some solace in the fact that Japan's still formidable kata-ized system is not impregnable. The Japanese are not unbeatable. They have their Achilles' heels. The solid phalanx they present to outsiders is part illusion. Penetrating the bulwark of their defenses—without the use of violence—is riot easy, however. It takes intimate familiarity with the system, obstinate persistence and a lot of patience.

The first break-through that most foreigners need to make in dealing effectively with the Japanese is to get beyond their formal manners—their visible kata. Their etiquette is seductively attractive to many Westerners, often impressing them to the point that they become entranced and lose some of their critical faculties, especially their ability to discern between form and substance. This alone is enough to account for many of the problems that foreigners have in relationships with Japanese.

Americans in particular are often susceptible to being overly influenced by stylized, elegant behavior, no doubt subconsciously relating such "good manners" to refinement and a high level of ethics and morality.

Another of the keys to breaching the social, political and economic walls surrounding Japanese is not to play the game on their grounds with their rules. If you choose to do things the Japanese way you have to be at least as good as they are just to achieve a tie. To win you have to be better than they are, and that is virtually impossible.

Dealing with Japanese on their playground and following their rules is invariably the long way, and often the wrong way. They have a clear advantage that generally allows them to control the situation and achieve their goals— or at least prevent outsiders from achieving theirs.

Japanese typically do not react to calls for fairness or equality in the Western sense—and this often appears to be the only strategy foreigners have in their dealings with Japan. There is no equality or Western style fairness in their hierarchical, exclusive system. Everyone is inherently unequal by design. Generally speaking, it is natural for Japanese to take advantage of people and situations when opportunities present themselves because that is exactly what they are conditioned to do.

It is therefore necessary for outsiders to deal with Japanese from a position of strength if they want to ensure a fair relationship. If you go in as a supplicant, and acknowledge your inferior position, you may get part or all of what you want but generally only if it serves the purpose of the Japanese. In this case, in is important for you to know what obligations you have really incurred and be prepared to fulfill them when the time comes.

Because the Japanese were not experienced in working with other people on an equal basis, as true partners, and at that point were psychologically unable to accept such relationships, most joint ventures between Japanese and foreign companies either failed completely after a few years or became disjointed, with the Japanese side actually running things.

Some of my most experienced—and candid—Japanese colleagues said at that time that there had yet to be *one* foreign-Japanese joint venture that has worked in the truest sense and spirit of the relationship. One long-time expatriate businessman in Japan observed: "You can work for the Japanese or they can work for you, but you cannot work *with* them."

These factors generally applied to all relationships with typical Japanese, but there were numerous exceptions on an individual as well as a company basis. Still, warned both Japanese and foreign consultants, the best approach in any proposed relationship is to take nothing for granted, presume that you will be taken advantage of if there is any opportunity, and follow the best advice available.

Sometimes the most effective strategy when dealing with Japanese who want something from you is to make no effort whatsoever to adapt to the Japanese way. This tends to throw them off balance, break up their line and weaken their defenses. This approach is more likely to work when your meetings take place away from their offices—and the further you are from their home turf usually the better off you are.

Generally the ideal approach in dealing with Japanese is a combination of Japanese etiquette and Western techniques. Japanese protocol is fine in helping to set the stage for meetings and negotiations. Exchanging name cards, bowing, polite talk, developing personal ties...all contribute to harmony and feelings of goodwill, and in fact are pleasant experiences.

If you are in a selling position, however, you generally must go well beyond what you would normally do in making business contacts with Western companies.

Japan's older generations are naturally passing away and the younger generations are taking over. Their mindset, behavior and expectations are becoming more and more like those of typical Americans and other Westerners.

As this cultural transition continues Japan may lose much of the power that has driven it in the past.

###

www.ingramcontent.com/pod-product-compliance
Lightning Source LLC
Chambersburg PA
CBHW021425170526
45164CB00001B/99